Tea Time Entertaining

DOLORES SNYDER

A COLLECTION OF TEA THEMES & RECIPES

1st Printing   4,000 copies

ISBN 0-9746872-1-9

Library of Congress Catalog Card Number
2003098468

FRONT COVER PHOTO BY
John Parrish

BACK COVER PHOTO BY
Gerald Davis

BOOK PHOTOS BY
John Parrish

INDONESIAN TEA PLUCKERS BY
Richard H. Snyder

FAIRY TEA INVITATION BY
Angela Galloway-Marshall

WIMMER
COOKBOOKS

ConsolidatedGraphics

1-800-548-2537
www.wimmerco.com

Dedication

*For Samantha, Lily, Ella and Luke ~
my grandchildren.*

Table of Contents

Foreword by Rodney Tyler

I first met Dolores "Dodie" Snyder in 1990 - on one of those blindingly-hot, sweltering days that only Texas seems to be able to manage adequately. Days when the dust going into your pores meets equal and opposite amounts of sweat coming out - and irritation of all kinds is the order of the day. Poor Dolores - she had agreed to put on a full English tea in the garden for us.

I was there with a photographer called Gerry Davis - whose picture taken that day graces the cover of this book - and the purpose of our visit was to produce, for an English Magazine, one of those articles, which poke gentle fun at our American cousins for their odd ways, yet at the same time point to some wider sociological meaning.

In this case, the very thought of a lady called Snyder from Dallas, Texas putting on English tea - or even considering herself capable of such a thing - was the amusing concept which had drawn us there. And the wider significance was that, to my English journalist's mind, her activities in teaching about tea and its ceremonial were indicative of a general resurgence of "old" values and manners, which seemed to be manifesting itself across America at the time.

It did not take long to realize that I had met my match on two counts - and that I was going to be producing a rather differently-shaded article from the one I had originally anticipated. As the temperature soared into the 100's, a seemingly endless succession of perfect cucumber sandwiches and smoked salmon sandwiches and egg-salad fingers and tiny tomato rounds, followed by perfect scones with clotted cream and jam, followed by divinely dainty fancies and a Victoria sponge cake and a Queen of Sheba Chocolate cake - all appeared in the calmest of professional order from refrigerators, ice boxes and beer-coolers - and were taken out into the garden.

There they were placed on a proper antique lacquered tea trolley, and on one of those collapsible, three-tiered "whatnot" tables, which women seem to be able to manage with ease - but which fold up as soon as men so much as look at them. And, in the broiling heat they were rapidly photographed before being offered - many of them as they visibly began to wilt - to the assembled party of female friends and neighbors, who had taken the trouble to dress immaculately for the occasion in a fine array of silk and cotton print dresses. All of this was washed-down with perfect infusions of Darjeeling and Earl Grey and China - served from antique teapots as old, almost, as our Empire itself.

It was magnificent. It was a tour de force. But that was not all. Then came the second blow to my upstart journalistic presumptions. This woman called Snyder, from Dallas, Texas began talking to me about the ceremony of English Tea. She told me the history of it and its role in the modern world. She told me where she had enjoyed it most. She talked me through the etiquette of it, where to serve it and to whom. She opened my eyes to the dozens of different types of tea you can give - and to cap it off, she had the audacity to tell me, an Englishman, how you should make the perfect cuppa. I learned a lot that day. Dolores Snyder knew it all. She was a walking encyclopedia.

I made the mistake - or the perceptive comment - of saying as much. And I gather this book is to some extent the result of that throwaway remark.

Over the years since that most fabulous of tea parties - and most fascinating of lectures, Dodie, her husband Dick and their family have become close friends with my family. And on each of the many occasions we have met, on both sides of the Atlantic, I have monitored the progress of the great tome. Now it is here, and it is every bit as interesting, every bit as comprehensive, every bit as authoritative - and every bit as mouth-watering - as it promised to be when she first talked to me all those years ago.

It is a wonderful book. Alas, there is only one thing missing ...... the real thing - the sandwiches, the scones, the cakes and the divine infusions. But, once you have read the book, you will be able to create that yourselves.

Rodney Tyler

Introduction

Growing up in south Texas, iced tea was the beverage of choice in my family but that was to change once I married a geologist who worked in many different countries. On our first visit to England, we took tea in an old mill in Surrey where the watercress was growing for our sandwiches. It was there I first fell in love with the ritual of the English tea. During the early 1970's, my husband's work took us to London for three years where we lived in an all British neighborhood on Pollard's Hill. We enrolled our son and daughter in the English schools and settled into the British habit of taking tea in the afternoon. I enrolled in the Cordon Bleu for cooking classes and took English historical walks with a wonderful Englishman. When we had to return to the USA, we traveled on the Queen Elizabeth 2 where we indulged in afternoon tea.

This tome had its birth twenty-five years ago when my daughter suggested I teach a class on A Proper English Tea. She said, "Mom, you entertain with it so well." We were in the middle of a gasoline shortage and my husband, ever the conservative geologist, said, "You won't have anyone come." I mailed my brochure telling my students about this new tea class to be held in my British friend's home overlooking Lake Dallas. Forty-five ladies signed up before a week had passed. I scheduled another class two weeks later. I think the reason taking tea took off is because Braniff Airlines had started their direct service to London and Texans wanted to learn how to pour a cuppa.

Twelve years passed and I continued to offer classes on entertaining with tea. In 1990 an article appeared in *The New York Times* about this lady teaching tea and etiquette in Texas. Rodney Tyler, a British journalist, saw it and contacted me about writing an article for *The Mail on Sunday*. He and Gerry Davis, the photographer, came out on the last day of July when our temperature outdoors soared to 100 degrees F. When they asked me if I would mind doing the photos outside, I said, "You've got to be kidding?" They were NOT! My friends who had come to be part of the tea party ferried cream cakes to the back garden where we braved the heat. After the photo session ended, the journalist said, "You have to write a book on tea and etiquette as we have nothing like it in England." My students had been asking me for just such a book. Realizing I had the recipes, I started in earnest to write about entertaining with tea.

In the beginning I had twenty-five themes from my years of teaching. I tried to market this book to the publishing houses that I felt would be interested. One suggested I revise the book and shorten it which I did. Then I finally got an agent who was really enthusiastic about it. She came up with the title *Tea Time Entertaining*. Realizing my passion for the subject of tea, my agent felt I should self-publish. When I lectured to The Smithsonian Associates, their enthusiasm for my book convinced me to do so.

For years, my students have been begging me to write about entertaining with tea and the social customs that accompany this ritual. During the 1990's, tea became a popular brew for business meetings and tea rooms began to spring up all over the country. Tea suddenly was the brew for health, too. I was asked to write an article on the health benefits of tea for a national magazine and it was reprinted in *The Saturday Evening Post*.

My recipes are easy to follow as I have incorporated my teaching methods. The themes I have included have proven to be popular with students. Recently, I have found younger students coming to my classes. They wish to entertain with tea and with careful preplanning, the recipes can be prepared in advance for a stunning table of tea time treats. With the etiquette of hostessing a tea, one can set the scene for the ambiance of A Proper English Tea at home. I wish I could share a cup of tea with you and become friends.

Five percent of the net proceeds from my book will benefit the educational charity, Teach for America.

Dolores Snyder

Tea Tales

Grandmother Hepburn's silver tea service on a galleried tray, her Victorian loveseat and barrel chair set the mood for a Victorian tea. A Staffordshire waste bowl and matching teacup in foreground, a fine Limoges sardine box and three-tiered silver plate tea butler displayed on a lacquered tea cart inlaid with soapstone chinoiserie combine for maximum sophistication with a tea bell to announce tea time.

Tea Tales

"Thank God for tea! What would the world do without tea? —How did it exist?
I am glad I was not born before tea."

Sydney Smith 1771-1845.

History of Afternoon Tea

We have three royal ladies in English history to thank for the custom of taking afternoon tea, as we know it today. When Catherine of Braganza married Charles II in 1662, she brought tea as part of her dowry and introduced the court to the pleasures of a cuppa. At this time tea was drunk in small Chinese porcelain cups for it was very expensive and only the rich could afford to imbibe.

The joy of afternoon tea was born in 1840 when Anna, the seventh Duchess of Bedford, decided to indulge in a 4 PM snack of bread and butter plus a pot of tea. In her era breakfast was served along with ale or mead to start the day. This hearty repast was meant to last until dinner, as lunch was not taken during those days. Anna grew faint from hunger in the late afternoon and remedied the situation with her tea pickup. Soon she added small cakes, tarts and friends to her afternoon sustenance in her boudoir. Her English friends took her habit of tea and conversation to the drawing room, lifting it to the ultimate with fine china tea services.

Queen Victoria enthusiastically endorsed this new ritual of afternoon tea with a passion and often baked the sweets herself for her Prince Consort. She realized that tea and its accoutrements of fine china and silver were good for the nation's economy. She even had Minton design a special tea service with the tartan of Balmoral castle. Queen Vickie was known to add whiskey to her cuppa regularly in her later reign.

Victorian England was ostentatious at the tea table with sandwiches, sausage rolls, tarts, fancy pastries and cakes soon supplanting bread and butter. This era gave birth to the social customs of tea etiquette that was brought to its zenith during the Edwardian period with the dance or tango tea. The tea dance was the rage until World War I and was revived in hotel ballrooms after the war. Now there is only one hotel in all of London that still observes this charming ritual with mostly tunes of American composers being played.

The custom of taking tea with dainty tea sandwiches, scones, tarts and fancy cakes was known as low tea and the privilege of only the upper classes that had servants. Low chairs and small tables were used in the drawing room. The hostess poured the tea from a silver teapot and passed the teatime treats, which the servant had prepared. Today " low tea" has evolved into afternoon tea and takes place around 4 PM.

High tea is the evening meal of the blue collar working person and is served between 6 to 7 o'clock. There may be two hot dishes such as kippers on toast or fish and chips to be followed by slices of fruity tea cakes washed down by cups and cups of tea. The tea is usually brewed in a teapot referred to as a brown betty. This meal is taken in the dining room seated in chairs around the dining table.

Personal Memorable Teas

*I*n 1969, I spent the month of June in the Hotel St. George in Algiers dining extremely well on French food. My geologist husband then took me to London where he left me at the Grosvenor House Hotel on Park Lane while he attended a conference in Brighton. The afternoon of July 1, I decided to treat myself to tea in the reception area of this bastion of English hotels. I was seated directly in front of a television set so that I might view the investiture of Charles as the Prince of Wales on his 21st birthday. He seemed so young as the plumage of feathers was placed atop his head.

Slowly I became aware that I was in fact witnessing two ceremonies—the one on television and the one taking place right around me. And each was very moving in its own way. I fell in love with the idea of tea, such a wonderful custom. I think we Americans love it because of the ritual with its own pomp and circumstance. It slows you down at a lovely part of the day and prepares you for the evening. My husband once wrote in my outline for this book that tea bridges the gap between lunch and supper as it is fortification for an assault on the pub (where he indulges in his favorite English bitter). Nevertheless he too enjoys tea, as do a lot of men, and often joins me in London at some hotel renowned for its teatime fare.

In the early 1970's my husband's work took us to live in London for three years. This gave me ample time to research the English tea custom in hotels, country tearooms and private homes. My most memorable tea came about through my husband's work when he met Buddy Fogelson, a Texas oil wildcatter, who was considering drilling in the North Sea. For lunch my husband took Buddy to his favorite pub for a steak pie and a pint of English bitter.

Several months elapsed and during our summer vacation in the U.S., Buddy invited us to his ranch, Forked Lightning near Sante Fe, New Mexico. It was there on the veranda I had my Earl Grey poured by his wife, Mrs. Buddy Fogelson, better known as Mrs. Miniver of the silver screen—Greer Garson. Our daughter and I sat enthralled as Greer introduced us to her Aunt Mary, upon whom she had modeled the part of Mrs. Miniver. With the charming British company, brilliant blue sky and fresh mountain air that tea will live with me forever.

For our fifth wedding anniversary my husband presented me with James Beard's **Treasury of Outdoor Cooking**, a 55-gallon drum barbecue barrel and a Steuben bowl for the center of the table. I cooked my way through that tome and nineteen years later when I took my first class with Beard, he chuckled when I handed him the worn volume and said, "I love to get a book in this condition."

Upon his death I was among those cooking to raise money to establish The James Beard Foundation in his Greenwich Village brownstone. One year my husband barbecued a whole pig and I prepared his garden vegetables. The next year I hosted a very successful tea-cooking seminar as a fundraiser.

This involvement with the Foundation led to my hosting a tea during the May Birthday Celebration of 1990 at The James Beard Foundation in New York City. I was cooking and brewing tea in my mentor's kitchen for sixty-five ladies and one gentleman that day. On the tea cart that afternoon were some of Beard's personal tea favorites as his mother was English and he observed the custom of daily afternoon tea. I hoped he was pleased looking down from that great tearoom in the sky.

In June of 2002 I was the featured English tea expert for The Smithsonian Associates in Washington, D.C. during their **Britain: Her History, Her Culture, Her Majesty** as part of Queen Elizabeth's Jubilee Year. I packed my trusty aluminum suitcase with my British tea memorabilia of antique china, silver and linens in order to set up a proper tea table and hand carried my lavender cartwheel tea hat. During my slide/lecture show, I demystified the brewing and serving of a proper cup of tea, recounted tea lore, and described the history of afternoon tea. I then answered questions from 176 ladies and gentlemen regarding the ritual of afternoon tea as they enjoyed my Victorian Garden Tea menu which the Willard Hotel executed perfectly. This tremendous response made me more determined than ever to publish this book for I knew I had an audience out there thirsty for the British ambience of tea time.

Tea in Today's World

Tea has become very popular in the States, especially on both the East and West Coasts. Business is now being conducted over cups of tea instead of cocktails as tea is the break that lifts without a later fall. A woman executive feels more comfortable conducting business over tea than in a smokey cocktail lounge. The "power tea" is fast replacing the power breakfast in the corporate world. After all, the business tea has its roots in the Chinese, Indian and Middle Eastern cultures.

Tea provides that healthful lift enabling one to think more clearly while easing tension. Cup-for-cup tea has less caffeine than coffee; a pound of tea produces around 200 cups versus 40 cups of coffee per pound. Caffeine-free teas are now available as well as herbal teas. Next to water, tea is the second most frequently drunk beverage in the world.

In the 1970's Chinese doctors in Yunnan conducted experiments in drinking Pu-Erh tea which showed it lowered cholesterol levels. French researchers in Paris repeated the Chinese experiments and found that drinking three cups of Pu-Erh a day for a month did indeed lower lipids as efficiently as the most advanced medicine, clofibrate. In 17th century England tea was drunk mainly for its curative powers for headaches, giddiness and heaviness, colds, dropsies, scurvies and was reputed to prevent infection.

In 1998, Dr. Mitch Gaynor, a cancer specialist at Cornell University's Strang Institute, reported that results of initial tests show that the antioxidants in tea inhibit the body's cells from becoming cancerous. In 1991 at a meeting of the American Chemical Society in New York City a report was presented that indicated green tea may prevent cancer of the skin, lung, liver and stomach. The tea leaves contain epigallocatechin-3-gallate, or EGCG, whose possible anti-cancer effect could be due to its reaction with "free radical" chemical groups. You must drink four cups of green tea a day for its cancer protective benefits. Another reason to drink green tea is the possibility that it inhibits dental cavities. Other studies indicate that tea strengthens the cardiovascular system.

"Tea, though it is ridiculed by those who are naturally coarse in their nervous sensibilities... will always be the favored beverage of the intellectual."

Thomas DeQuincey 1785-1859.

Through my years of conducting tea classes, I have found my students asking questions about the ritual of the English tea with its genteel formality. They find it a most pleasant way to entertain with a return to the elegance of social rules that emphasize the ceremony of a bygone era. With the recent surge in popularity of things Victorian, taking tea has also received a boost. I emphasize to my students that it is a most inexpensive way to entertain for both small and large groups within a specified time and have your guests feel they have experienced something very special.

A Historical Tea Time Line

2737 BC   Emperor Shen Nung is credited with the discovery of tea when some leaves of a nearby wild tea plant floated into his bowl of boiling water. He noted the change in color and liked the taste, declaring it a medicinal drink.

794-221 BC   Zhou dynasty used tu (tea) in religious rituals.

725 BC   Cha, the Chinese word for tea, appears.

780   Lu Yu wrote *Ch'a Ching* (The Classic of Tea), ten books on tea from planting, plucking the leaves, processing, twenty-five utensils for making and serving tea. A Taoist, he wrote how to appreciate tea as an art…"Goodness is a decision for the mouth to make."

805   Tea is introduced into Japan.

1191   Eisai, a Zen Buddhist, brought tea seeds from China. He authored the first Japanese book on tea.

1452   Murata Shuko founded the ceremony of tea known as chanoyu.

1500	Yx-ing potteries produced stoneware teapots for the "kung-fu" tea ritual.
1591	Sen-no Rikyu, who perfected the Japanese tea ceremony, commits suicide.
1610	Dutch bring the first tea from Java to Europe.
1657	East India Company imports the first tea into London. Thomas Garraway's coffeehouse offered tea to its customers who came to Exchange Alley.
1662	Catherine da Braganza marries Charles II and brings tea as part of her dowry; introduces the court to green teas served in small blue and white porcelain tea bowls without handles.
1665	Sugar is used to sweeten tea.
1684	Tax on imported tea results in the English consuming more smuggled tea.
1689	Russia trades furs to the Chinese for tea.
1698	Milk is added to brewed tea.
1700	A Tea Party painted by Nicholas Verkolje.
1703	J.F. Bottger makes a red teapot at Meissen.
1707	Fortnum & Mason was established in London.
1708	The United East India Company is a merger of the two East India companies.
1709	J.F. Bottger perfects the production of white porcelain.
1717	Thomas Twining opens The Golden Lyon in The Strand in London where ladies could purchase their favorite tea.
1742	Ranelagh Gardens opened in Chelsea for tea and entertainment.
1751	The Worchester Royal Porcelain Works is founded in England.
1756	The Sevres porcelain works is founded in France.
1765	Josiah Wedgwood designs a dinner set for Queen Charlotte and becomes potter to Her Majesty.
1767	The British Parliament passed the Townshend Revenue Act which taxed tea imported into the Colonies. The Colonists smuggled tea in from Holland.
1770	John Singleton Copley paints Paul Revere with his globular teapot.

1773	The Tea Act retained a tax of threepence a pound on tea. "They have no idea that any people can act from any other principal but that of interest; and they believe that threepence on a pound of tea, of which one does not perhaps drink ten pound in a year, is sufficient to overcome the patriotism of an American," Said the great tea lover, Dr. Benjamin Franklin.
1773	Samuel Adams organizes the Boston Tea Party. A group of men, disguised as Mohawk Indians board the East India Company Ships in Boston Harbor and dump 342 chests of tea overboard.
1774	Subsequent tea parties followed in New York and Annapolis, resulting in the birth of a new Republic.
1774	Josiah Wedgwood perfects Jasper ware, used in tea ware.
1778	A wild tea plant was found growing in Assam, India. The East India Company was looking for an area in India in which to grow tea.
1800	Spode invented bone china resulting in fine teapots.
1800-1812	John Jacob Astor, Stephen Girard and Thomas Handasyd Perkins became America's first millionaires dealing in tea and trade with China.
1837	Queen Victoria becomes Queen of England and embraces the custom of tea.
1839	First tea from Assam comes to England and is sold at auction. This is black tea, which becomes popular with tea drinkers.
1840	Duchess of Bedford introduces afternoon tea to her friends.
1851	Crystal Palace opens as part of the Great Exhibition.
1856	Darjeeling tea gardens had its first plantings of tea.
1870	Ladies began wearing tea gowns.
1876	Thomas Lipton opens his first grocery in Glasgow.
1879	Mary Cassatt paints The Cup of Tea.
1880	Mary Cassat paints Lydia at Afternoon Tea and The Tea.
1883	Mary Cassat Paints The Lady at the Tea Table.
1887	Queen Victoria celebrates her Golden Jubilee, fifty years on the throne.
1889-1890	Mary Cassat paints The Tea.

1890	Thomas Lipton becomes a tea merchant; buys Ceylon coffee plantations and turns them into tea estates. Sells his tea at a lower price under his logo.
1890-1891	Mary Cassat paints The Visit.
1894	The Lyons chain of tea shops is established in London.
1897	Queen Victoria marks her sixty years on the throne with the Diamond Jubilee.
1903	Willow Tea Room by Charles Rennie Mackintosh, opens in Glasgow.
1904	Richard Blechynden pours hot Indian tea over ice at the St. Louis World's Fair and Americans fell in love with it.
1908	Thomas Sullivan sends samples of tea to his customers in little silk bags.
1909	Thomas Lipton begins marketing his tea in the United States.
1925	Clarice Cliff designs her Bizarre tableware decorating teapots with vibrant colors.
1952	Queen Elizabeth II ascends to the throne of England.
1800-2000	The Dudson Group, potters in Stoke-on-Trent, celebrate their bicentenary with a visit from the Queen. Eighth generation of family ownership.
2002	Queen Elizabeth celebrates her Golden Jubilee.

Tea Etiquette

Dolores Snyder

Fairy Tea
to honor

Samantha June Snyder
Sunday June the ninth
Four o'clock
3409 Hidalgo
Irving,
Texas

RSVP 972-717-4189

Fairies adorn a violet teapot announcing
a tea for my first grandchild, Samantha June, with
an Austrian teacup of brewed Darjeeling.

Tea Etiquette

"There are few hours in life more agreeable than the hour dedicated to the ceremony known as afternoon tea."

Henry James 1843-1916.

Why Have Tea

*T*he popularity of the British afternoon tea has been on the rise during the past decade and will continue its ascent as more Americans discover the gracious customs associated with taking tea. Enjoying hotel teas across the nation has resulted in hostesses serving afternoon tea at home. A business woman I know now uses it to entertain her clients and finds they enjoy it much more than a lunch. It is a civilized way to recharge one's batteries leaving one both relaxed and uplifted.

Guidelines For A Proper Tea

*T*he invitation for afternoon tea may be as informal as a telephone call a week ahead or a printed invitation issued three weeks prior to tea time. The time may be anywhere between three and six o'clock but four to six is the ideal.

Delicate finger sandwiches, scones with jam and clotted cream, and a cake form the basic menu for a small informal afternoon tea. As the guest list increases, items such as shortbread, tea breads, tarts, pastries, fruity loaf cakes and trifle swell the menu. Be it informal or formal, presentation of the food is of the utmost importance.

The tea table or tea tray should be covered with a starched embroidered or lacy cloth and a small vase of flowers, even a single rosebud. This is the time to use your prettiest porcelain teacups and saucers with teaspoons and small plates with an embroidered napkin between each. The china does not have to match and is more interesting if you have a collection of different violet or rose patterns. Silver will be a knife plus a pastry fork. The teapot, porcelain or silver, will be in the center of the table along with a jug of hot water, a slop bowl for spent tea leaves, a tea strainer, a milk pitcher, sugar bowl with lump sugar and tongs, and slices of lemon on a plate with a lemon fork for those guests who prefer it rather than milk in their tea.

The sandwiches, scones and cakes with servers may be on the teacart, space permitting, or on a small side table. I employ sugar tongs to pick up sandwiches. Two to twelve guests are the ideal number for an intimate tea which usually is served in the living room with a roaring fire in winter. The patio could be the setting in spring or summer when the garden may be enjoyed.

For the formal tea reception of twenty to one hundred, buffet service is in order with organization the key to success. The dining room table can be laid with cups and saucers at one end where the tea will be poured from a silver teapot. It is best to use a tea concentrate and have a large server of hot water over an alcohol burner. The concentrate is poured into the teacup and filled with hot water. At the opposite end of the table a tea punch may be offered. Usually the hostess asks close friends, for whom it is an honor, to man these stations while she circulates among her guests. Domestic help removes the spent china teacups and plates.

The table is centered with flowers and surrounded by an array of tempting tea time treats. Sandwiches are placed on doilies or starched napkins and may be garnished with fresh herbs or flowers. Scones may be split, topped with jam or fresh berries and lavished with clotted or whipped cream. Tarts are displayed on three-tiered servers and cakes on elevated stands. Plates with napkins between each and cake forks should be on both sides of the centerpiece. A sideboard may also supplement the groaning array of sweets.

The ritual of the tea service is observed more rigidly in the informal tea rather than the formal buffet affair. You, as hostess, pour a cup of tea for each guest and inquire as to their preference for milk or lemon and with sugar or not. Each guest has her tea at hand and her small plate before the sandwiches are passed. Once the sandwiches are finished, then you offer the scones with cream and jam. Now, it is nice to have fresh plates for the cake as the used plates have become pretty sticky. Fresh cups of tea are in order about this time.

Tea Time Customs

From London hotel teas to the French pastry tea, the Russian evening tea, the Japanese tea ceremony, the Chinese gong fu ritual, the Middle Eastern sweet mint tea and the business tea of the United States, there is a world of options for this versatile brew. Wherever I travel, I make it a point to take tea the native way for a cultural discovery.

Europe

London Hotel Teas: For the ultimate experience of an English hotel tea, one must book in advance for a table at The Ritz where a naked golden nymph fountain presides over the Palm Court lounge. The pale pink light is very flattering to a lady's complexion; you may wish to wear a hat for you really are on view. If you have a gentleman joining you, he must wear a jacket and tie. The marble tables are high and the chairs were designed to be sure you sit up very straight. The tea fare of freshly made finger sandwiches, scones baked that afternoon, pretty cakes and French pastries will cost you a substantial sum but you will be one of the elite for two hours of enchantment.

Taking tea at The Mandarin Oriental Hyde Park Hotel has the park in view and you will see equestrians riding by as you sip your Earl Grey. The Savoy Hotel, that grand old lady of The Strand, has tea set in the Thames Foyer with art deco mirrors, murals and trompe l'oeil garden paintings. My husband enjoyed the tea fare so much, he asked for seconds and they were served promptly with a smile. An Edwardian gem, The Waldorf Hotel, specializes in tea dances on the week-ends so you must reserve to be a part of the tango and fox-trot scene. All the tunes are American so you will feel comfortable as you two-step. Even my non-dancing mate twirled me around the dance floor. For the feeling of tea in an English manor house, have tea at Brown's Hotel where the apple strudel is a winner and seconds are expected. My personal favorite is the Basil Hotel where I once glimpsed Lady Di as she joined a wedding reception for her former flat mate. My husband rates their sardine sandwiches the best in town.

French Tea Salons: The fancy tea room or *salon de thé* of France may be enjoyed at Angelina in Paris where Marcel Proust and Coco Chanel sipped tea regularly. Once a Viennese tea salon and later named for the owner's daughter, this institution has been officially designated a historical landmark. The murals, skylight, gilded mirrors, green marble tables and "Louis XV" chairs have aged with elegance. Unwind here after a visit to the nearby Louvre.

Several French tea salons serve lunch with tea time being observed from 3:30 to 5:00 PM. The French patisserie of chocolates, madelines, tarts and sorbets are a gastronomic treat to be savored as I discovered on a tour of Parisian tea salons where the French were definitely at table. Laduerée is one not to be missed for their chocolate macaroons which were chosen number one by the Club des Croqueurs du Chocolat. The black marble tables are the smallest ever and set very close together happily resulting in a conversation with your French neighbor. With its pale olivewood boisserie, turn-of-the-century decor, the cherubs floating among the clouds overhead baking croissant under the sun's rays, it provides a theatrical background for the chic Parisian women with their designer shopping bags filled from the showrooms on the rue St. Honoré. A Priori Thé is located in one of Paris's glass-enclosed passages from the nineteenth century and is becoming a tea salon where the French preppies congregate. After walking the rue de Rivoli, you may wish to take tea with a book. Try the upstairs tearoom of W.H. Smith, one of the best-stocked English language bookshops in the City of Light.

Fans of the French pastry shops may have tea along with their specialties. Millet is famous for its almond financier; Dalloyou serves its celebrated Gateau Opera; La Maison du Chocolat creates chocolate treats to satisfy any chocoholic's dream. Christian Constant, on the left bank, is a salon /patisserie famous for its pear mille-feuille. Should you tire of pastry teas, splurge for a caviar tea at Le Petit Boule, near the Ecole Militaire, where there are delicious piroshki. Above Caviar Kaspia, located on the place de la Madeleine, you may opt for smoked sturgeon and caviar with a blini and sour cream.

The French demand quality teas, and the Mariage Frères tea salon has the finest selections from China, India, Ceylon, Japan, Siam, Indonesia, Pakistan, Nepal, Vietnam, Russia, Turkey, South America, Australia and New Guinea. At Mariage the tea is brewed in a china pot with a silver insulator. Classical music is appropriately played in this setting of natural wood trellises and pale yellow beige walls. I had the best tea fare of open-faced sandwiches, especially the circle of chicken salad with foie gras. Their scones come with a smoky tea jelly. Be sure to visit the tea museum on the second floor. Mariage is a refreshing stop after touring the museums situated in the Marais neighborhood.

Verlet, an 1880 tea shop, is an interesting place to have tea. You are squeezed among the tea canisters and the bags of coffee beans so the ambience is one of a market stall.

Russia: Tea became the beverage of choice in Russia during the 17th century with camel caravans of tea being brought from China. The Russians now cultivate their own tea but also import tea from India. They serve tea as a strong essence from the teapot and they dilute it with hot water from the spigot of the samovar, an urn with a chimney of burning charcoal. Samovars may be made of brass, copper or silver with elaborate carvings and scrolled feet. Antique ones are very collectible. The teapot is placed on top of the samovar which is at the right side of the hostess. The brew is drunk from a bowl or glass set in a filigreed metal holder with a handle. A slice of lemon might be added and rose petal jam for the sweetener. Another way to sweeten this strong tea is to hold a sugar cube between the teeth and sip the hot tea through the cube. This may explain why the Russians I have been hosting for the past two years have so many gold teeth in the front of their mouths.

Chaikhana is the Russian name for a tea house where the men take their tea. A tea in the home might be accompanied by pirozhki, a dumpling pastry made from yeast or short pastry dough and filled with cabbage, cottage cheese, mashed potatoes or cooked fruit. Prior to Lent, a Bliny Tea with stacks of blinis topped with sour cream, caviar, smoked salmon, red salmon roe, smoked sturgeon or pickled herring washed down with cups of strong black tea would fortify one for the fasting to come.

Asia

*C*hina: The Chinese initially practiced the rituals of boiled cake cha, or tea, in the T'ang dynasty, whipped tea in the Sung dynasty, and steeped tea during the Ming dynasty. Emperor Kiasung (1104-24) was a champion of tea and wrote a *Treatise on Tea*.

On my first trip to China in 1983, I discovered the Chinese do not consume tea during their meals, but after and between, and conduct business over cups of tea. During my visits to medical centers, I was given a large lidded cup of tea with tea leaves in the bottom. This cup was continually filled with hot water for successive cups of tea over a period of two hours. The Chinese savor the fragrance and taste of their teas much as a wine connoisseur. They believe food interferes with the true taste and appreciation of fine teas.

On a recent visit to Hong Kong, I visited the Flagstaff House Museum of Tea Ware, which is part of the Hong Kong Museum of Art. There I viewed pictures of the gongfu tea ritual, a custom that began in the late 18th century during the Qing dynasty. It is still practiced today in the provinces of Chaozhou and Fujian. There are nine steps to a perfectly brewed cup of tea. A miniature teapot of Yixing clayware is filled three-fourths to the top with Oolong tea. The thimble-sized cups are without handles and are placed in a ceramic bowl that stands on a tray. The kettle of boiling water is poured over the tea and immediately the teapot is emptied over the cups. This washes the tea leaves and warms the cups. The teapot is refilled with hot water and the cups are emptied onto the tray. After steeping for about thirty seconds, the tea liquor is poured in a circular motion over the cups whose interior is white to better show the color of the tea. The entire infusion is poured into the cups. Two more infusions are made once the first is drunk. Several years ago, a student brought me two sets of these miniature teapots and cups from Taiwan.

In Hong Kong, tea in the Clipper Lounge of The Mandarin Oriental hotel is offered British style with a selection of fifteen teas and infusions. The set afternoon tea arrives on a three-tiered silent butler. Business deals are being finalized over tea and tiramisu or crème brûlée. The women are stunning in Chanel suits or Hong Kong copies—hard to tell. This is a power people watching scene and a vast contrast to taking tea in mainland China.

Tibet: Tea in Tibet is served with salt instead of sugar and yak butter is mixed into the brew in place of goat's milk. They use brick tea which is a combination of black and green teas. When they wish to brew it, the tea is shaved from the brick which weighs two to four pounds. The tea is served in bowls filled to the top.

> *"It is in the Japanese tea ceremony that we see the culmination of tea ideals.....It is a religion of the art of life."*
>
> *The Book of Tea* by Kakuzo Okakura, 1906.

Japan: Although the Japanese were drinking tea in the eighth century, it was not until the twelfth century they adopted the whipped tea ceremony from the Chinese. Eisai Zenji, a Buddhist monk, traveled to China to study the Zen school. He returned with the tea ritual of the Sung which evolved into the Japanese tea ceremony. Rikyu, the Tea Master in the 16th century, developed the rules of purity, harmony, respect, simplicity and tranquility for the tea ceremony. He created the tea room (sukiya), which is nine feet square and accommodates five persons. The mizu-ya is the storage room for the tea utensils. The guests wait in the machi-ai, a separate room, connected to the tea room by the roji, garden path. The tea room is very simple but very clean and is adorned with only an Ikebana flower arrangement or a scroll painting.

After a gong sounds, the guests enter, one by one, through a low doorway and the host follows. The guests sit cross-legged on straw mats and are served by the host. A charcoal brazier, furo, is sunken in the middle of the tea room. The tea kettle, okama, has pieces of iron arranged in the bottom that produce a melodic sound when boiling. Three scoops of green tea are placed in a glazed bowl, the chawan. Matcha is the powdered green tea which is whipped to a liquid jade froth with a special bamboo whisk, chasen, after the boiled water is added by using a bamboo dipper, hishaku. Once the tea and water mixture is whisked, the guest of honor sips from the bowl first, praising the tea's taste and aroma. After two more sips, he wipes the edge of the bowl with the silk napkin, kobukusa, and passes it to the next guest. After all the guests have sipped the strong tea, the host brews a batch which he serves in tea bowls.

Harmony is the essence of the ceremony. Guests speak quietly during the tea ceremony and admire the art and beauty of the ritual. A light meal (kaiseki) may be served prior to the tea ceremony or only sweets (wagashi) with the second tea. The host departs with the tea equipage and the guests remain to chat or may also depart. A simple ceremony of only tea will be approximately forty five minutes while the one with elegant food may be as long as four hours for the emphasis is upon the harmony of color between the food and the dishes upon which it is served.

Thailand: Tea leaves were steamed and formed into balls to be eaten before they were ever used as a beverage in Siam. Today many herbal infusions are drunk in addition to teas. There is a special salad of pickled tea leaves that originated in Burma. On a recent trip to Bangkok, I had tea in the Authors's Lounge of The Oriental Hotel. The conservatory, once open to the tropical sky, now has a fiberglass skylight draped with multi-color silk sheer fabric. The walls are white washed stucco and pale blue fretwork tops the white doors. White wicker chairs and love seats have pale green elephants on the linen upholstery. The tea trays rest on top of white wicker elephants. Hanging baskets of flowers and orchids are in abundance. Bamboo is growing in enormous containers set on the marble floors.

You have your choice of thirteen different teas from the classics to Monkey Picked. Three sugars, granulated, brown and white rock crystal are offered along with milk. Newspapers and books are there for your reading pleasure. A flute and guitar provide a soothing background for this setting. At any moment, I thought I might be joined by Noel Coward, Joseph Conrad, Alec Waugh, Graham Greene, S. J. Perelman, James Michener, Tennessee Williams, Gore Vidal and John Le Carre, who have sipped tea here.

India: The Indians brew their chai, or tea, very strong, and sometimes flavor it with cardamom seeds or fennel. They serve it with sugar and milk in cups and glasses. Tea stalls are brewing throughout the day. Tea is welcomed when traveling by train where it is served on board and at stations along the way. The beverage is served in a clay cup which one breaks upon consuming the tea.

Middle East

Iran: Tea is the national drink. Flowers and herbs are often added to the black tea which is served hot and sweet in cups or glasses. The ghavakhane is a tea house where men gather for entertainment. A storyteller recites the **Book of Kings,** the history of Persia's earliest rulers.

My first taste of green tea with spearmint was in North Africa where it accompanied a pigeon pie, bastila, which was made of phyllo pastry and sweetened with sugar and cinnamon. The tea, brewed in a brass pot with a long slender spout, was poured from a great height, which cools the tea and produces a foamy brew, into clear glasses. I found it to be extremely delicious with the meal. In Morocco, the sweet mint tea is served by men as is the Muslim custom. A guest must drink three glasses from weakest to strongest. Sometimes a dash of rose water is added to the mint tea in Tunisia. The Egyptians drink their black tea very sweet but without milk in small glasses. The samovar is used in Turkey much as in Russia. Herbs and tisanes are to be found throughout the Middle East. The Yemenites brew a tea from the leaves of a narcotic shrub known as kat.

Australasia

*I*n the cities of Australia, the British custom of tea prevails but out in the bush country, a bushman has a "billy can" in which he boils the tea with the water. This produces a very strong, hearty brew to which he adds sugar and a gum tree leaf for flavor. In the "back blocks" of New Zealand, the tea leaves are boiled with the water.

United States

*T*he Dutch introduced tea into the Colonies in the seventeenth century and the British immigrants brought their custom of tea with them. When England levied a heavy tax on tea, the colonists rebelled against taxation without representation. The Boston Tea Party in 1773, a patriotic protest against the tax on tea, turned the colonists into a nation of coffee drinkers. This was the beginning of the American Revolution. In the nineteenth century, the Yankee Clipper ships brought tea from China, Ceylon, and India. If you are a maritime fan, visit the Peabody Maritime Museum in Salem, Massachusetts for an informative explanation and display of the tea trade. During the twentieth century, the United States became a nation of iced tea drinkers.

For the past decade, there has been a return to having tea in the afternoon and conducting business over a cup of vintage Darjeeling. The power tea during which executives discuss deals costs less than a business lunch and tends to be quieter. Oak paneled walls and comfortable club chairs contribute to a more relaxed setting. Some firms even have their own tea caddies and samovars, not just for clients, but to enjoy a soothing respite during the hectic afternoon.

New York City: Tea in the Astor Court of The St. Regis is a luxurious experience with a diverse choice of twenty-four black, green and oolong teas or six herbals for sipping as you relax in this pink and gold room. The china has a bouquet of rosebuds with gold ribbon trim and the silver tea butler is filled with sandwiches, the lightest scones and miniature sweets. You may finish with a glass of champagne as you gaze at the trompe-l'oeil clouds and mythological murals painted by Zhuoshu Liang that surround the sparkling chandelier overhead.

The Tea Box Cafe in the basement of the Takashimaya department store offers a Bento Box of beautifully presented cold food. Their Fanciest Formosa Oolong is an amber liquid with elegant peach flavor. Chocolates from Bernadou are tempting as are the antique Japanese teapots offered for sale. The draped white ceiling and beige table and chairs are a quiet background for the creative fare. Whether you prefer traditional blends of tea, do try some of the new flavored or scented teas and the herbal infusions. There are caffeine-free teas available for healthier drinking. Be adventurous and even blend your own. Sam Twining once said to me, "Having tea restores our batteries leaving us reasonable and safe to drive or do a sport."

Tea Accoutrements

Setting a proper tea table is a reflection of your personal style for entertaining. Collecting the accoutrements can be an educational journey as antique dealers are willing to share their knowledge.

From Russian teapot atop a brass samovar to silver tea service with slop bowl, tea accoutrements span a wide range of materials and size. Black lacquer Dutch tea caddy, 1820, houses two varieties of tea in its dual pot metal canisters next to Mason's ironstone Mandarin tea caddy and brass toasting fork. Ready for use are a Victorian sugar shaker and silver pieces include tea infusers, tea strainer, toast rack, sugar tongs, lemon fork, 1810 English caddy spoon and teaspoon. Displayed on a tea cloth with a hand crocheted border of teapot, teacups and 4 o'clock, the proper time for afternoon tea covering a round tea table.

Teapots – Silver was used for the first British manufactured teapots and one by Hester Bateman is a jewel to collect. Those of pottery and porcelain came later in the shapes of cottages, monkeys, cauliflowers and even human heads. Josiah Wedgwood produced black basalt stoneware ones as well as Queensware, the cream colored earthenware and jasper ware. Other manufacturers of tea ware were Spode, Coalport, Copeland, Minton and Rockingham. Paul Revere made the neo-classic design silver teapot.

Tea Cosy – A padded cover for a teapot that is often quilted or crocheted to keep the tea hot but is to be removed once the desired strength is reached or the tea will develop a stewy taste.

Tea Urns – Silver Georgian ones with an elaborately decorated elongated body standing on four feet were used for the Waco Historical Society Tea where I was the guest lecturer. A spigot was at the bottom and two handles for carrying with a domed finial contributed to the beauty of these.

Tea Samovar – The Russian utensil made of copper or brass, designed to keep water hot with a center tube for charcoal and a spigot for dispensing hot water.

Tea Kettle – Modern ones are electric but antique ones are sterling silver or Sheffield plate with a trivet on which it stood with a spirit lamp underneath.

Tea Caddies – Containers for storing tea. The early ones were part of the silver tea service and later wooden ones with inlaid designs with two compartments and a center section for lump sugar or mixing the teas.

Caddy Spoons – The early ones were made in the shape of a shell as the Chinese included a natural scallop shell for measuring the tea.

Teapoy – A three-legged table that has been fitted with canisters and mixing bowls.

Tea Table – An antique Georgian one covered with an embroidered cloth and napkin.

Infuser – Stainless steel or ceramic ones in which the tea leaves are placed for the brewing time and removed once the tea is brewed.

Tea Strainers – A bowl-shaped strainer that is placed over the cup to catch any stray leaves. May be silver, silver plate or porcelain with a stand on which it rests.

Mote Spoon – A rare piece of silver that skims off any stray tea dust and has a spike handle for unclogging the teapot spout of leaves.

Teacups and Saucers – A china tea service consisted of twelve cups and saucers with a cake or scone plate, lidded sugar bowl, milk jug and teapot to match. Rosebuds and flowers were often the decoration.

Milk Jug or Creamer – Made of porcelain or silver. Those shaped like a cow with a hole in the middle of the back and a spout in the mouth are prized collectibles.

Hot Water Jug – Made its appearance in the nineteenth century.

Sugar Bowl, Sugar Tongs and Teaspoons – For cube sugar with the tongs being first made in the late seventeenth century as were the teaspoons.

Slop or Waste Bowls – The dregs of tea from strainers were deposited in these.

Tea Services – A silver galleried tea tray with a teakettle and its spirit burner, a sugar bowl, a creamer, the hot water jug, slop bowl and strainer comprise the Victorian or Regency tea service.

Lemon Fork – A two-pronged silver fork for spearing lemon slices.

Tea Butler – A three-tiered server in silver plate for serving sandwiches, scones and pastries.

Jam Jar and Spoon – Sets of two are often made of crystal and come with a silver plate stand on which the spoons hang.

Clotted Cream Bowl and Spoon – A small crystal or ceramic bowl with serving spoon.

Butter Knife, Bread-and-Butter Plate and Pastry Fork – Became part of the tea service in the nineteenth century. The pastry fork has a sharp edge on one side.

Cake Stand – A pedestal elevated plate for displaying tea cakes.

Muffiner – A shallow silver dish with a domed lid to keep English muffins hot once they are toasted.

Tea Types and Proper Brewing

The tea pluckers, in their exotic batiks, in the misty tea gardens of Indonesia, take a break from the arduous chore of picking the leaves with the help of long fingernails grown for this purpose.

Tea Types and Proper Brewing

"The first cup of tea moistens my lips and throat. The second shatters my loneliness."

Chinese mystic of the T'ang Dynasty.

History of Plant

The Chinese were the first tea drinkers about 5,000 years ago when their Emperor Shen Nung, who drank only boiled water, noticed some leaves from a wild tea plant had floated into his kettle. The resulting brew had such a pleasant fragrance and flavor, he continued to enjoy this accidental concoction.

Tea is made from the Camellia Sinensis, an evergreen plant with dark shiny green leaves that, if left unpruned, would reach a height of 40 to 45 feet. However, the tea industry decreed these bushes should be grown to no more than three to four feet. Tea bushes produce 100 years or more and are very hardy plants that grow from sea level up to 7000 feet or more. Three years after a cutting is rooted and put into the ground, it will be three more years before it produces. Plants grown from seed may be transplanted to the tea garden in six to eight months. Tea bushes are grown in low-lying tea gardens and contoured up steep hillsides with constant pruning to produce a compact bush. Some plants are allowed to grow unchecked to produce shade for the garden.

Tea is grown in a climate of tropical sunshine with abundant rain and flourishes best in an acid soil but it also is grown in sub-tropical areas. China, Formosa, Japan, Ceylon, India, Pakistan, Indonesia and Cameroon are the major producers of tea. Russia, Malaya, Mauritius, Burma, Siam, Turkey, Iran, Argentina, Brazil, Peru and Uganda also grow tea for the international market.

In the early part of the twentieth century, there were 105 acres of tea growing in Wharton County, Texas on the land of Shanghai Pierce, a legendary cattleman. After his death, his nephew carried on his tea growing plans and had plants for 500 more acres ready to plant when the Colorado River flooded and destroyed them. The only other tea presently grown in the United States is on Wadmalow Island, near Charleston, South Carolina. William Hall, a professional tea taster, and Mack Fleming, a tea horticulturist and former Lipton Tea employee, bought the tea research station when Lipton decided to close it down. They now produce tons of American Classic Tea on their Charleston Tea Plantation.

The first flush, plucking of the leaves, is the most prized and brings the highest price in the market, be it public auction or private sale. A framework of bamboo poles is placed over the plants and the plucking of two leaves and a bud commences the harvest. Women with small, slender fingers and long nails are the most skilled at plucking. The thumb and index finger pluck the leaves and are tossed over the worker's shoulder into a basket held in place by a band on the forehead. A plucker can remove up to sixty pounds of tea a day and is paid by weight at the end of the day with a wage of a little over a dollar. Four pounds of plucked tea leaves results in one pound of finished tea. In Russia, tea is harvested with a mechanical tea plucker but on the estates of the best teas grown on steep terrain, this would not be possible. On some estates the harvest goes on year round but on others, the plucking may be done only three or four times a year.

Once the tea is harvested, it is processed by withering which takes place on the upper floor of the factory. The green leaves are spread out to dry under a net with a blower fan to reduce their moisture content which takes six to twenty-four hours depending on the humidity. The next day the leaf is taken down to the ground floor where a rolling machine breaks up the leaf cells and produces a twisted red wet moss. The leaf is then broken up by ball-breakers, vibrating sieves, that separate the leaf so it ferments evenly. The leaf is taken to a room where it is spread out to ferment and it changes to a copper color. Then it is put on trays which move into a tea dryer where blasts of controlled hot air stop the oxidation.

The leaf is sorted and graded into Leaf and Broken. The Leaf grades are Orange Pekoe, Pekoe and Pekoe Souchong and the Broken grades are Broken Orange Pekoe, Broken Pekoe, Broken Pekoe Souchong, Fannings and Dust. Orange Pekoe denotes the size of the largest leaf. If done correctly, the tea is now ready for brewing but it will taste terrible because the black tea we drink is carefully blended to produce tea of consistent quality and taste.

Blends

Tea is very complex in flavor with a variety of tastes often compared to wine. Black Teas are in the red wine category with Oolong the white wine and Red Teas in the rosé category. This was demonstrated to me when I had the privilege of assisting the chief tea blending manager for Lipton's, who educated me about the processing and tasting of the tea leaf. After telling me that a tea taster serves an apprenticeship, usually with his father, I asked him how he became one. He informed me he was looking for a job after World War II and applied when he saw an advertisement in the paper—a lucky opportunity for him.

In our tasting he had seven pure unblended black teas to be sampled. Each sample weighed the equivalent of two old sixpenny pieces, 6.5 grams, on a scale and was placed in a special white china mug with saw-toothed edges on one side and a lid. The copper kettle, filled with fresh cold water, was brought to the boil and I poured the same amount into each mug. The tea was brewed for exactly six minutes and then poured into a bowl and I added a teaspoon of skim milk to show the true color of the tea. The serrated mug strained out the infused leaf and the lid with the infused leaf was reversed on top of the mug. This allowed the taster to see the infused leaf along with the dry leaf. He had a brass tasting spoon, or rather a "slurping" spoon, which he used to scoop up a spoonful of the tea and he sounded as if he were tasting wine by sucking the tea on to the back of his palate. After he had tasted for a few seconds, he spit into a gaboon. He was looking for certain characteristics in the dry leaf—clean, even—, the infused leaf—bright, green —and the liquor—,full, malty. In his thirty plus years of tasting up to several hundred cups of tea a day, he could even identify from what elevation on what estate the leaf had grown at what time of year. He was a true connoisseur of tea tasting.

India is the largest producer of Black Teas with tea gardens on the Himalayan border that produce Darjeeling, the "champagne" of black teas, and the Northern region of Assam, a brisk tea, with Nilgiri, a light tasting tea, in south-western India. I recently had an exquisite second flush Darjeeling designated as SFTGFOPl, Special Finest Tippy Golden Flowery Orange Pekoe premiere quality, from the Castleton estate. The muscat aroma was intense without being overpowering. I savored this flavor experience at Mariage Frères in Paris. The price of 100 grams was approximately $40, but it was a taste treat.

Black Teas are grown on tea estates in Ceylon, the second largest producer of tea in the world, with 70% being grown at altitudes over two thousand feet. China produces Black Teas but is more famous for its Green Teas, as is Japan. Green Tea is steamed and then fired resulting in a truer taste of the leaf. Formosa produces semi-fermented teas in the Oolong family.

Herbal & Floral Teas

Herbal and floral teas, or tisanes, may be brewed by adding a portion of the fresh or dried herbs, pesticide free, to tea leaves or they may be brewed with the herb only in the same way as tea is brewed. These infusions have become very popular with the younger generation, especially in France, for the pure herb teas have no caffeine. Some of the herbs have been used for medicinal infusions with the ginseng root recommended for impotence. My mother brews parsley tea every day for she swears it prevents bladder infections. Lemon verbena, mint, rosemary, borage, and chamomile are some of the herbs for potions with flowers and fruit adding flavors to black teas. Although we think of flavored teas as relatively new, the Chinese were adding fragrance to their teas in the seventh century, according to **Ch'a Ching,** a tome on tea authored by Lu Yu. China's Green Tea and Formosa's Pouchong are impregnated with the flavor of jasmine blossoms.

Another popular scented tea is Earl Grey, named for the second Earl who was given the tea by a Chinese mandarin after his envoy saved the mandarin's life. The secret recipe has been claimed by both Twinings and Jacksons of Picadilly. The distinctive flavor is derived from oil of bergamot, a citrus tree of the Mediterranean. This tea is the world's most popular blend today.

White tea, one of the most expensive Chinese teas, comes from the flower buds and leaves of the "Big White" bush. It is very pale in color with a sweet, subtle taste. The processing differs from black, green and semi-fermented teas, in that the leaves are only withered and dried.

Flower buds are often in teas but the fragrance is derived from the teas being sprayed with the essence of the particular flower. Lipton's tea taster told me that Constant Comment was an accidental discovery when some orange peel and spices were left with the tea which quickly absorbed the scents. Therefore, tea must be kept tightly sealed in order to preserve its taste and freshness.

Tea must be stored in an airtight tin so no sunlight, heat or moisture can enter. Black teas may be stored for up to a year and green teas no longer than six months.

Black, Green, Oolong and Scented Teas

Black Teas

Black Teas—can be taken with milk, lemon, or sugar.

India Black

Assam—a bright-colored liquor that is full-bodied with a malty taste. Excellent for breakfast served with milk.

Darjeeling—a delicate tea with a Muscatel flavor sold in different grades but only connoisseurs seek out first and second flushes. Drink in the afternoon plain or with milk. Use for iced tea as well.

Nilgiri—a bright, brisk tea not often found on its own as it is used in blends.

Ceylon Black

Orange Pekoe—a delicate tea with a smooth flavor. Name is the size and type of leaf, not color. An afternoon tea to be served with or without milk and makes excellent iced tea.

Flowery Pekoe—a flavorful full tea with golden tips in the blend.

China Black

Earl Grey—a scented blend of China and India black teas with a delicate fragrance of oil of bergamot. A favorite afternoon tea to be served with or without milk. Wonderful with sweets.

Keemun—brilliant red liquor with a mild, sweet flavor, often referred to as the burgundy of teas. Grown in Anhui province. Serve in the afternoon, with or without milk. Excellent when iced.

Lapsang Souchong—a large-leaf tea with a distinctive smoky flavor produced by smoking the tea in large baskets over oak or pine chips. A brew that you either like or dislike due to the smokiness. The best comes from the Fukien province. Serve hot without milk and iced, with lemon.

Yunnan—a large-leaf golden liquor with an exquisite aroma and a long lasting taste on the palate. A newer tea from the Yunnan province marketed since 1949. Serve hot without milk.

Green Teas

Green Teas—can be drunk without milk or sugar.

Gunpowder—a yellow-green fragrant liquor made from pellet-looking shapes of unfermented leaves produced in China's Anhui province. It is used to make mint tea in North Africa and Turkey. World's oldest known type of tea that was used as a means of currency.

Silver Dragon—a light liquor with intense aroma and a sweet taste. Has a silvery white down on its leaves.

Sencha—a pale green liquor with a fresh, flowery taste from Japan. Low in tannin.

Gyokuro—a greenish liquor with a rich, herbaceous taste that lingers on the palate. Expensive.

Matcha—a jade liquor from the powdered leaf. The tea used in the Japanese tea ceremony. Excellent in sauces and ice creams.

Oolong Teas

Oolong Teas—are meant to be tasted on their own.

Imperial Oolong—an amber liquor with a fragrance of ripe peaches. Comes from the Fukien province in China and is known as Black Dragon, the finest of teas. Drink with or after an Oriental meal. Makes wonderful iced tea.

Grand Pouchong—a golden liquor with a delicate aroma and a subtle flavor. Low in caffeine. Excellent evening tea.

Jasmine—a pale heady liquor with a refreshing fragrance that comes from the dried Jasmine flowers. Drink in the afternoon or evening. Excellent iced.

Scented & Flavored Teas

China Rose, Lychee, Imperial Russian, Cinnamon and Spice, Apple, Black Currant, Vanilla, Apricot, Passion fruit, Lemon, Peach, Orange and Violet are just a few of the scented and flavored teas that have become so popular. At the Mariage Frères in Paris, I counted 12 Earl Grey blends, 9 different Jasmines, 8 traditional perfumed blends, 57 fantasy blends and 44 perfumed blends for a total of 130 scented and flavored teas. I chose the Earl Grey Silver Tips, Passion fruit and Violet for a taste experience.

Several blends have been created for the "Royals". The Prince of Wales for Edward VII, Her Majesty's Blend for Queen Victoria, Queen Mary and Lady Londonderry are some examples. Coronation Tea was a special blend for Queen Elizabeth. A recent new one is Queen Catherine Blend for Catherine of Braganza.

Tea Equipage

"Now stir the fire, and close the shutters fast, Let fall the curtains, wheel the sofa round, And while the bubbling and loud-hissing urn Throws up a steady column, and the cups That cheer but not inebriate, wait on each, So let us welcome peaceful evening in."

William Cowper—1786

The first teapots came from Yi-Xing, near Shanghai, and were small, unglazed red or brown stoneware and the teacups were the size of thimbles, for tea was expensive and drunk only by the affluent Europeans in the 16th century. Later cups were small, translucent porcelain bowls, without handles, and deep saucers which were often used to cool the tea. The English added the handle in the mid-eighteenth century. The Chinese blue and white willow pattern which tells the love story of Koong-tse and Chang was a most popular import for a tea service which would be comprised of the teapot, sugar bowl, milk jug, teacups and saucers.

Josiah Wedgwood developed a cream colored earthenware that Queen Charlotte liked so well, he named it Queensware. He produced tea ware for the masses in glazed stoneware. Besides this famous Staffordshire potter, there were potters at Chelsea, Worcester, and Derby. Josiah Spode created the first bone china and his firm later produced the Balmoral pattern in honor of Queen Victoria. The hot water jug, the slop bowl in which spent tea leaves are deposited, the bread-and-butter and tea plates became part of the tea equipage in the nineteenth century.

In the eighteenth century English silversmiths added to the accouterments of tea with silver tea services. A footed, galleried silver tray to protect the table surface, the silver teapot, sugar bowl and milk pitcher, sugar tongs, tea knives and fork sets, tea strainers and tea caddies were all manufactured for the wealthy but with the advent of silver plating, the production of silver tea services became affordable for the masses.

The Malayan word kati, a measure of 1.2 pounds, became caddy in English. Tea was imported into England in caddy tins or terracotta jars. The British soon were fashioning caddies in mahogany, rosewood, satinwood and glass with a lock and key to prevent servants from pilfering their precious tea. An elaborate caddy would have three compartments—two for black or green teas and a third for mixing the teas. Chinese export caddies were made in silver, lacquer, tortoise shell and carved ivory.

Caddy spoons were used to measure the tea and the first was a scallop shell which the Chinese included with their tea. The English silversmiths soon were fashioning caddy spoons in many shapes and sizes. A silver mote spoon with its perforated bowl was designed to remove any foreign leaves from the brewed tea while its spiked handle would be used to unclog the spout of the teapot, jammed with leaves. Both the caddy and mote spoons, along with the sugar nips, were kept inside the tea caddy. Silver caddy and mote spoons have become antique collectibles for their intricate workmanship.

Tea kettles which were kept warm over a spirit burner or candles were made in sterling silver or Sheffield plate and the tea urn with a spigot were all part of the tea table. I recently had the pleasure of viewing a neoclassic silver teapot by Paul Revere. It was to be auctioned at Christie's and the estimated price was $60,000 to $80,000.

The English tea table with its carved rim and claw-and ball feet is a work of art to behold. However, a Philadelphia Chippendale tilt-top pie crust tea table, 1760-1775, attributed to the carver Hercules Courtenay, set the auction record at Christie's in 1986. It sold for $1,045,000., the first American piece to break the million dollar mark.

During the Victorian period, afternoon tea was a period of considerable sustenance and more accessories became a necessity. The folding three-tiered cakestand, nests of three tables and tea trolleys were added. The teapoy on its pedestal of three feet would be a caddy standing by.

Brewing the Perfect Cuppa

I once read that tea is flavored water but what flavor depends on brewing the "perfect cuppa". Whether you are brewing black, green or oolong tea, certain guidelines are to be followed. Select a teapot made of porcelain, silver, glass, stainless steel, pewter or earthenware—the English "Brown Betty" is a personal favorite—but never aluminum as tea and aluminum quarrel silently producing a dark bluish color, almost black, and a foul tasting tea. Check the spout for dripless pouring and, if made of metal, be sure the handle is insulated. The lid should stay in place when pouring.

A clean teapot is another prerequisite for tea loves cleanliness but do not use detergent or bleach to remove tannin stains. Use two tablespoons of baking soda and pour in boiling water to clean the teapot. Let it stand for three hours and rinse well. Sam Twining parted with this cleaning method in a tea seminar I attended.

Always rinse out the kettle before filling it with fresh, cold water. If your water is high in mineral or salt content, buy bottled spring water. Fortnum & Mason of Picadilly in London will analyze your water and select a tea blend right for it. Fill your teapot with hot water from the tap for a degree of temperature is critical for proper brewing. Bring the water in the kettle to the boil but do not allow it to continue to boil for the oxygen in the water will be deflated, resulting in flat tasting tea. Tea loves oxygen and needs it to develop its maximum flavor.

Empty the water from the teapot and add one teaspoon of loose tea per cup and one for the pot. Bring the teapot to the kettle and pour on the boiling (212 degrees F.) water. Place the lid on the teapot and steep the tea for three to five minutes, depending on the type of tea in the infusion. Green tea brews at a water temperature of 185 degrees F. and requires a minimum of three minutes; a medium leaf black tea must steep for five minutes and oolong, a large leafed tea, takes up to seven minutes. Remember, some teas brew light in color while others produce a dark brew. The brewing time is known as the agony of the leaves.

If using a stainless steel or ceramic tea infuser, remove it after the steeping time is completed. In using an infuser, only half fill it to allow for the leaves to expand. I have a cotton strainer that fits down inside the teapot and I remove it after the brewing time has lapsed. Some teapots come with a built-in strainer but they must be deep enough or they only work when brewing a full pot. Special filters are available for brewing tea and may be removed once the brewing time has been reached. If using tea bags for a pot of tea, the brewing time is shortened for the smallest grade of tea leaf, known as dust, is used in the bags. Once the tea is brewed, remove the infuser, or place a strainer over the cup when pouring. Some purists advocate straining the infusion into another warm teapot, but I feel this lowers the tea's temperature. In either case, stir the tea before pouring. Have a jug of hot water at hand to dilute the tea if asked.

Once the tea infuser has been removed, a tea cosy may be placed over the teapot to keep the brew warm. A tea cosy is a padded cover that is embroidered, quilted and often made of velvet or satin. Cosies come in many different guises and I have seen a quilted one in the shape of an English cottage. If used with tea leaves still in the pot, a stewy taste of tea results because the brew takes on a strong bitter taste.

Left top to bottom: Chinese tea caddies beside a Mason's Blue Pagoda tea bowl, circa 1816, with an 1850 eagle cup plate, Adams blue jasper sugar bowl with silver cover and Victorian Indian Tree pattern breakfast cup, oriental tea cups and a Blue Willow wedge shaped cheese keeper, Wedgwood Portland blue 1890 cheese keeper with Muses & Trees'.

Skim milk shows the flavor of the tea at its best for the hot tea slightly "cooks" the milk. Never use cream for the tannin in tea will curdle the cream. Sugar numbs the palate and the taste of the tea but my British neighbors always offered it and often used it themselves. Offer white cube, or granulated, sugar and lemon, if desired.

One can decaffeinate tea by pouring on the hot water to cover the leaves and leaving it to brew for 30 seconds. Pour off the first brew immediately and 95% of the caffeine has been removed. Now pour fresh water over the leaves and let the tea steep for the required amount of time.

When I lived in London, our house came with a gardener for whom I always made tea. He preferred it with milk but no sugar. At the beginning of June, I carried his mug of tea down to the bottom of the garden and he said, "Mrs. S. it is summer and I take lemon in my tea in the summer." He was wearing a sweater as it was a very gray day with a brisk wind blowing. I proceeded to return to the kitchen to brew him a proper cup of summer tea with lemon but no milk!

The tea bag was a result of an enterprising American named Thomas Sullivan who sent samples of tea to his customers in handsewn silk bags. They tried to unsuccessfully brew a cup of tea and he switched to a gauze material. By the 1930's a special paper was used but today a special filter paper, which imparts no taste to the tea, has been developed. After opening a package of tea bags, store them in a tightly sealed container. They will keep up to a year and loose tea up to two but tea is at its best when fresh so purchase it in small quantities and try different blends. Be adventurous and create some blends of your own.

Growing up in south Texas I was, first, a drinker of iced tea long before I discovered the English ritual of an afternoon cuppa. We have an Englishman, Richard Blechynden, to thank for this refreshing drink. Richard was manning a booth at the St. Louis World's Fair in 1904, to promote the tea of India. The summer heat was oppressive and people were not in the mood for a hot cup of tea. In desperation, he poured his tea over ice in tall glasses and the public loved it.

Iced tea is usually made with tea bags but do try it sometime with loose tea using either Ceylon or Darjeeling for a crystal clear liquid. As ice dilutes the tea, you must allow for this by making it double strength. To six teabags, add 4 cups of freshly boiled water and steep for five minutes. Strain the tea into a quart pitcher and add cold water.

Today there are large tea bags which are the equivalent of three regular cup-size tea bags. Another popular way of brewing is to place the tea bags in a glass container and set it in a sunny place where the sun's rays do the brewing. The same can be accomplished by placing the covered container in the refrigerator overnight. Three large tea bags placed in a gallon jar filled with cold water make one gallon of iced tea. Always remember to remove the tea bags once the tea is made.

Sometimes when you refrigerate tea, it becomes cloudy. You can restore its clear color by adding a small amount of boiling water. Iced tea is usually served with a slice of lemon and a sprig of mint and sugar. A very popular canned version of iced tea has different fruit juices added for flavor. Iced tea even comes in a powder form that dissolves instantly in cold water which is convenient as is the mix with lemon or sugar. I find these great for taking along on picnics but I still prefer to brew my iced tea when at home.

Christmas Tea

Violet Tea

Earl Grey Imperial

St. James Restaurant Blend

Pu-Erh

Ceylon, Pettiagala

Assam, Napuk

Darjeling,
TGOP Princeton

Sencha, Honyama, Japan • Lung Ching, Dragonwell, China • Budding Jasmine Rose, China

Mutan White, China

Ti Quan Yin,
Oolong, Fujian

Dong Yang Don Bai,
China

Displayed with an antique brass tea scale from England with Tegor weights and a scorpion caddy spoon.

A Tea Guide

Black Teas
(fermented, are to be drunk plain or with milk or lemon)

Health Benefits: Strengthen immune system, promote digestion, inhibit growth of bacteria in mouth.

- *Darjeeling,* a delicate tea with a muscatel flavor, often referred to as the champagne of teas.

- *Earl Grey,* a scented blend with a delicate fragrance of oil of bergamot.

- *Ceylon,* a delicate bright tea with a smooth flavor. Excellent for iced tea.

- *Keemun,* a sweet-flavored red liquor, often called the burgundy of teas.

- *Lapsang Souchong,* a large-leaf tea with a distinctive smoky flavor produced by smoking the tea over oak or pine chips. Serve hot without milk.

Green, White and Yellow Teas
(non-fermented, to be drunk plain)

Health Benefits: Rich in vitamin C, selenium (prevents aging), and fluoride; lower blood pressure, promote digestion.

- *Gunpowder,* a fragrant yellow-green liquor made from pellet shapes of unfermented leaves produced in China. Used to brew mint tea in North Africa and Turkey.

- *Lung Ching,* also known as Dragon's Well, a fragrant jade liquor made up of leaf buds with a sweet taste.

- *Yin Zhen,* or *Silver Needles,* a white liquor of delicate sweetness from Fujian. Plucked two days a year when the leaves resemble silver needles; expensive, but contains no caffeine or tannin.

- *Sencha,* a clear green liquor rich in vitamin C.

Oolong Teas
(semi-fermented, to be drunk plain)

Health Benefits: Help lower cholesterol and high blood pressure.

- *Grand Puchong Imperial,* a delicate liquor, of an amber hue with a smooth, sweet taste.

- *Ti Kuan Yin,* an amber liquor, the taste and aroma of ripe peaches.

Traditional Tea Menus

The glory of a summer garden is reflected in
the highly unusual left-handed silver tea service with a
three-tiered silver-plated stand displaying tea fare on a
19th century heirloom quilt. Dancing maidens decorate
etched iced tea glasses beside an Art Deco pitcher.

Garden Party Tea

A garden party tea on the lawn is a wonderful setting for christenings, graduations or baby showers with the little ones in attendance. Tables may be covered with antique quilts whose colors have mellowed with time. Hanging baskets with blooming plants and birdcages filled with flowers make attractive table settings. Ask the ladies to wear long cool, even antique, dresses and large straw hats to ward off the sun. Be sure to keep refrigerated food in coolers until serving time for you want it to be appetizing in appearance. By arranging several serving dishes in advance, your fare will not have a tired, wilted look. To keep sandwiches from drying out, cover them with damp paper towels topped with plastic wrap.

Garden Party Tea

Smoked Salmon with Herbed Cheese Triangles

Queen Adelaide's Chicken and Ham Spread
on Whole Wheat Fingers

Egg and Cress on White Bread

Tomato Rounds on White Bread

Mini-Scones with Berries and Whipped Cream

Lemon Curd Tarts

Petticoat Tails

Queen Mother's Favorite Cake

Ceylon Tea

Strawberry Tea Punch (page 178)

Smoked Salmon with Herbed Cheese Triangles

4	ounces smoked salmon
8	ounces cream cheese, softened, divided in half
1	teaspoon capers
2	tablespoons fresh dill
2	scallions, chopped
1	clove garlic, minced
2	tablespoons, red bell pepper, minced
2	tablespoons parsley, chopped
24	thin slices extra-thin whole wheat bread

❀ In food processor or blender, place salmon, half of cream cheese, capers, dill and scallions. Process until smooth and remove to a bowl. In another small bowl, beat remaining cream cheese with garlic, bell pepper and parsley.

❀ Spread 8 slices of bread with salmon mixture, top each slice with second slice and spread third slice with herbed cheese and place on second slice. Now you have a triple-decker sandwich. Wrap in plastic and refrigerate 30 minutes to firm up filling. To serve, trim crusts from each sandwich and cut into 4 triangles.

Yields: 32 triangles.

The herbs and the peppers add not only flavor but color to this sandwich filling.

Queen Adelaide's Chicken and Ham Spread Fingers

4	ounces unsalted butter, softened
1	teaspoon tomato puree
½	teaspoon curry powder
1	teaspoon grated orange rind
½	cup ground chicken breast
½	cup ground cooked ham
¼	cup cream
1	green onion, minced
20	slices extra-thin whole wheat bread
	Salt and freshly ground white pepper

In bowl, combine butter, tomato puree, curry powder and orange rind. Mix chicken, ham, cream and onion in a bowl. Spread 10 slices of bread with the curry butter and spread remainder of slices with the chicken and ham filling. Sandwich together, decrust and cut each sandwich into 4 fingers.

Yields: 40 fingers.

This filling was reputed to be a favorite of the Queen's Prince Consort, King George IV.

Egg and Cress on White Bread

6	hard-cooked eggs
¼	cup mayonnaise
	Salt and freshly ground white pepper
1	bunch watercress, washed and dried
20	slices extra-thin white bread
4	ounces unsalted butter, softened

❀ Once the eggs are cooked, plunge them into ice cold water and crack their shells. This facilitates easier peeling and also deters the black ring forming around the yolk. Chop the eggs roughly and mash the yolks and whites together in a bowl with the mayonnaise. Add salt and pepper to taste.

❀ Spread the bread with the butter and top half of the slices with the egg filling. Top with watercress and press bread slices together. Decrust and cut each sandwich into 4 squares. Garnish with the watercress.

Yields: 40 squares.

A classic sandwich filling that has a peppery taste due to the watercress but the taste may be varied by the substitution of mint.

Tomato Rounds on White Bread

1   **pound large tomatoes, peeled, deseeded, chopped finely**

Salt and freshly ground white pepper

4   **ounces unsalted butter, softened**

10   **slices white bread**

Fresh parsley for garnish

❁ Drain any liquid from tomatoes by placing them in a mesh strainer. Place chopped tomatoes in a bowl and season with salt and pepper.

❁ Spread bread with butter and cut out rounds that are 1½-inch in diameter. Top with tomatoes and a bit of parsley.

Yields: 40 rounds.

Note: Small grape tomatoes may be sliced and arranged on the bread rounds.

If you are able to buy an unsliced loaf of sandwich bread, remove the crust and slice it lengthwise ½-inch thick. I once had a surfeit of yellow tomatoes from my garden and found they were delicious topped with a thin slice of cucumber.

Mini-Scones with Berries and Whipped Cream

1	teaspoon unsalted butter to grease baking sheet
4	cups unbleached all-purpose flour
5	teaspoons baking powder
1	teaspoon salt
4	tablespoons granulated sugar
	Grated rind of 1 lemon
4	ounces cold unsalted butter, cut into 16 equal pieces
1	large egg, beaten
1	cup skim milk plus 1 tablespoon for glaze
1	box fresh berries of choice, washed and drained
1	cup whipping cream

❀ Preheat oven to 425 degrees F. Lightly butter a baking sheet. Sift flour, baking powder, salt and sugar together into a large mixing bowl. Use your fingers or a pastry blender to cut in the butter. Beat egg with the 1 cup of milk and stir quickly into the flour. The dough must just hold together; check to feel that it is not too wet or dry. You may need a tablespoon or more of milk. Do not overwork the dough or your scones will be tough.

❀ Turn out onto a floured work surface and pat out to 1½-inch thickness. Cut out circles with a 1½-inch round fluted pastry cutter that you dip in flour. Be sure to cut straight down and do not twist the cutter. If you do, your scones will not rise evenly. After the first scones are cut, gather up the scraps and gently press them together for a second cutting. Place on baking sheet ½-inch apart and paint tops with the 1 tablespoon of milk to glaze the scones.

❀ Bake in center of oven 10 minutes or just light golden in color. Remove to a wire rack to cool and place a tea towel over the scones to keep them moist.

❀ Remove any stems from berries. Whip cream. Split scones with fork. Place a heaped teaspoon of whipped cream on top of each scone half and top with the fresh berries.

Yields: 40 halves.

Note: Clotted cream is fresh milk with a high butterfat content that is heated slowly in a heavy saucepan but never allowed to boil. The pan is covered and once cool placed in the refrigerator. The next day one may skim off the clotted cream.

Scones are always split and spread with the jam first followed by clotted cream, a wonderful British dairy product I first experienced at a Devon cream tea. If clotted cream is unavailable, I serve my scones with whipped cream. During the fresh berry season, I lavish the scone with the cream and top this off with raspberries, blueberries or strawberries.

Lemon Curd Tarts

Lemon Curd:

4	lemons, grate rind and juice
4	ounces unsalted butter
1	cup granulated sugar
5	large eggs, beaten

Pastry:

2	cups unbleached all-purpose flour
⅛	teaspoon salt
½	teaspoon baking powder
4	ounces unsalted cold butter, cut into 16 equal pieces
1	tablespoon sugar
¼	cup ice water
1	teaspoon lemon juice

Lemon curd, also known as lemon cheese in England, is wonderful as a spread on muffins, crumpets, and as a filling for cakes. It is so addictive, I never have it on hand. You may store it in the refrigerator for up to two weeks. The pastry I use came from a cooking class a French pastry chef taught for me and it may be used immediately.

❦ In the top of a double boiler, combine lemon juice and rind, butter and sugar. Place over simmering water, stirring to dissolve sugar. Slowly beat in the eggs. Cook, stirring every 3 minutes, until mixture thickens and coats a wooden spoon. Remove from heat and strain into a bowl. Cover the surface with plastic wrap and refrigerate.

❦ Preheat oven to 375 degrees F. Place flour, salt and baking powder into food processor bowl fitted with steel blade. Process to blend. Scatter the butter evenly over the flour. Process until mixture is size of peas.

❦ Dissolve sugar in ice water and add lemon juice. With processor running, pour the water mixture down the feed tube. Process just until the pastry comes together. Do not form a ball or pastry will be over processed and tough.

❦ Remove dough from processor to floured work surface and use your hands to bring it together into a smooth ball. Roll out with floured rolling pin to a thinness of ⅛-inch. This produces a crisp crust.

❦ Cut pastry with a 1½-inch fluted pastry cutter and place in mini-muffin pans. Prick bottoms with the tines of a fork. Bake with a blind of parchment paper or foil, cut to fit inside the tarts and filled with dried beans, rice or pie weights. Bake for 10 minutes, until golden brown, and remove from oven. Tarts will easily lift out of the pans. Cool on wire racks.

❀ To assemble tarts, use a teaspoon to fill with lemon curd or a pastry bag fitted with a plain ¼-inch tip. Tarts may be garnished with a fresh raspberry or blueberry for color.

Yields: **6 dozen tarts.**

Note: Pastry may be frozen and defrosted in refrigerator.

Petticoat Tails

½	**cup rice flour**
1½	**cups all-purpose flour**
8	**ounces unsalted butter, softened**
½	**cup granulated sugar**

❀ Preheat oven to 300 degrees F. Line a large baking sheet with parchment paper and draw 3 (7-inch) circles.

❀ Sift flours together onto wax paper. In mixer bowl, cream butter and sugar at medium speed until light and fluffy. At low speed, slowly add the flours. Mixture will be crumbly but do not over mix. Turn out on floured surface and knead lightly.

❀ Form the dough into 3 smooth circles on the parchment circles. I use a fluted pastry ring. To use a wooden shortbread mold, flour it and press dough into the mold. Refrigerate for 30 minutes before turning out onto parchment paper.

❀ Lightly score each round into 8 triangles. Prick evenly with a fork. Bake in center of oven for 30 to 35 minutes or just until shortbread starts to pale in color.

❀ Remove from oven and leave for 10 minutes to firm up. Transfer to a wire rack to cool. Use a serrated knife to cut through the scored lines.

Yields: 24 triangles.

Note: Flavor shortbread with ½ teaspoon ginger and 1 tablespoon finely chopped preserved ginger for a taste sensation. Dough may also be formed into a round as for cookies and refrigerated until firm. Then slice into ¼-inch thick slices for a cookie presentation. Dough freezes well.

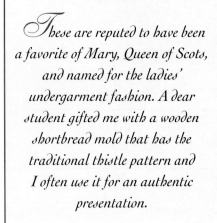

These are reputed to have been a favorite of Mary, Queen of Scots, and named for the ladies' undergarment fashion. A dear student gifted me with a wooden shortbread mold that has the traditional thistle pattern and I often use it for an authentic presentation.

Queen Mother's Favourite Tea Cake

Cake:

8	ounces chopped dates
1	cup boiling water
1	teaspoon baking soda
2	cups self-rising flour
½	teaspoon salt
6	tablespoons unsalted butter
1	cup dark brown sugar
1	large egg, beaten
1	teaspoon vanilla
½	cup chopped walnuts

Topping:

½	cup plus 2 tablespoons dark brown sugar
4	tablespoons unsalted butter
¼	cup cream
½	cup chopped walnuts

A friend in London sent this recipe when I requested an outstanding tea cake for Christmas. Above the recipe, the following was written, "The Queen Mother requests that this recipe should not be given away, but sold for 10p and the money given to a charitable organization." She must have raised a tidy sum by now for this typifies the sticky, dark English tea cake.

❀ Preheat oven to 350 degrees F. Grease and flour a 9 x 12-inch baking pan, shaking out any excess flour.

❀ Soak the dates in the cup of boiling water with the baking soda. Let this stand while mixing other ingredients.

❀ Sift flour with salt onto wax paper. In mixer bowl of electric mixer, use the paddle to cream the butter until light in color. Add the brown sugar, half a cup at a time, and beat until fluffy. Beat in the egg and vanilla with a tablespoon of the flour.

❀ Strain out the date liquid and save it to add last. Add the soaked dates and the walnuts to the creamed mixture.

❀ Fold in the flour, half a cup at a time, alternating with the date liquid. Spoon batter into the prepared pan and bake for 35 to 40 minutes. Remove from oven and let cool in pan.

❀ For topping: Place sugar, butter and cream in a heavy-based saucepan and bring to the boil. Boil, stirring for 3 minutes. Spread over baked cake. Top with the chopped walnuts. Cut cake into 1½-inch squares.

Yields: 4 dozen squares.

Victorian Tea

The Victorian tea table would be ostentatiously laden with sandwiches and sweets as the tea time menu reached its zenith during Queen Victoria's sixty-four year reign. After a visit to her daughter in Russia, the Queen brought lemon slices to the tea menu. Up to that time tea was drunk either white (with milk) or black. The brewed tea should be served from a silver teapot or a fine porcelain one for taste. Queen Victoria endorsed blends of tea named after the royals.

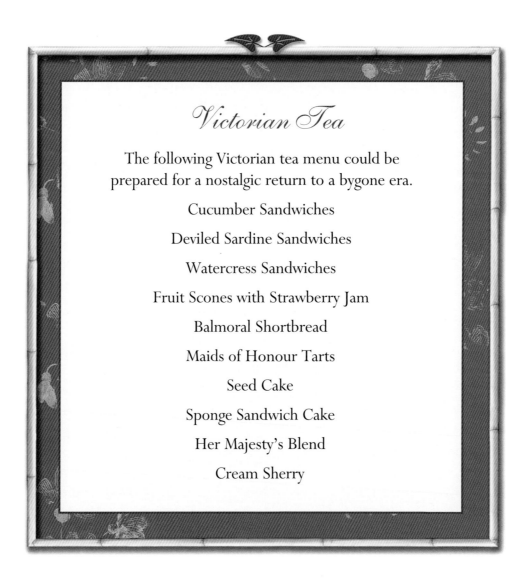

Victorian Tea

The following Victorian tea menu could be prepared for a nostalgic return to a bygone era.

Cucumber Sandwiches

Deviled Sardine Sandwiches

Watercress Sandwiches

Fruit Scones with Strawberry Jam

Balmoral Shortbread

Maids of Honour Tarts

Seed Cake

Sponge Sandwich Cake

Her Majesty's Blend

Cream Sherry

Sandwiches

*T*he invention of the sandwich is attributed to the fourth Earl of Sandwich who was such a compulsive gambler that he could not tear himself away from the gaming tables long enough to eat. He made do with a slice of meat between two pieces of bread but such a hearty sandwich is inappropriate at tea time.

Sandwiches for the tea table are to be made from the thinnest of breads with a good crumb. Bread purchased the day prior to its use produces the best sandwich. A small bread and butter knife is used to spread the softened butter and filling. A bread knife with a serrated blade is employed to decrust the sandwiches before cutting into triangles, fingers, squares or rounds.

Cucumber Sandwiches

10 **slices extra-thin white sandwich bread**

4 **ounces unsalted butter, softened**

2 **burpless English cucumber, scored with a fork and thinly sliced**

❀ Spread bread thinly with the softened butter. Arrange 4 to 5 slices of cucumber on 1 slice of bread; top with other buttered slice. Decrust and cut into triangles.

Yields: 20 triangles.

*D*o not be tempted to salt the cucumber slices or your sandwiches will be soggy.

Deviled Sardine Sandwiches

5	ounces sardines in olive oil, drained
4	tablespoons butter, softened
1	tablespoon Dijon mustard
2	tablespoons lemon juice
1	teaspoon Worcestershire sauce
	Salt and freshly ground black pepper
1	tablespoon finely chopped gherkin pickle
1	tablespoon finely chopped celery
10	slices thin brown bread
4	ounces unsalted butter, softened
1	tablespoon chopped parsley for garnish

Put first 6 ingredients in blender. Blend until light and creamy, adding up to 1 tablespoon of the drained olive oil. Stir in chopped gherkin and celery. Spread bread with the butter and then the sardine filling on 1 slice only. Sprinkle sardine slice with parsley. Sandwich together, decrust and cut into fingers. Open-face fingers may also be made by cutting bread into fingers and then spreading with the butter and sardine spread. Use boiled sieved egg yolks for garnish.

Yields: 20 fingers.

My hostess at Hampton Manor in the Cotswolds of England served this recipe as a filling for hollowed-out lemon halves as a first course. Men love it as a sandwich filling.

Watercress Sandwiches

2   bunches watercress, washed and
    dried well

8   ounces unsalted butter, softened

20 slices extra-thin white sandwich
    bread

1   tomato

❀ Pick twenty of the best watercress sprigs for these will peek from the ends of the rolled up bread slices. Remove the leaves from the remaining watercress stems.

❀ Place the butter in a blender and add the watercress leaves. Blend and remove to a bowl.

❀ Decrust the bread and roll with a rolling pin to flatten it. Spread bread with the watercress butter and roll up.

❀ To serve, insert watercress sprigs on one end and place in a circle on round serving tray with the watercress sprigs on the outside circumference of the tray. Carefully peel tomato in one continuous piece to form a rolled tomato rose and place in the center of the sandwiches for garnish.

Yields: 20 rolled sandwiches.

This could be called a double watercress sandwich for the butter is enriched with chopped watercress. Rolling the bread before spreading it with the butter makes it more pliable.

Fruit Scones

1	teaspoon unsalted butter to grease baking sheet
4	cups all-purpose unbleached flour
5	teaspoons baking powder
1	teaspoon salt
¼	cup sugar
4	ounces cold unsalted butter
¼	cup golden raisins
¼	cup dried currants
1	large egg, beaten
1¼	cups skim milk

❈ Preheat oven to 425 degrees F. Grease a baking sheet. Sift the flour, baking powder, salt and sugar into a large mixing bowl. Cut the butter into 8 equal pieces and rub into the flour mixture with the tips of your fingers until mixture resembles large peas. Toss in the raisins and currants.

❈ Make a well in the center of the mixture. Combine egg with milk and pour all but 1 tablespoon into the well lightly mixing with fork until mixture just comes together.

❈ Turn out onto a floured board and pat out to ¾-inch thickness. Cut into 2-inch rounds without twisting the cutter. The first scones cut are the most tender so stamp them out as close together as possible. Gather the trimmings together and repeat cutting process. Place on baking sheet ½-inch apart and paint tops with reserved milk.

❈ Bake for 10 to 12 minutes or just until tops are golden. Remove to a wire rack to cool.

Yields: 18 scones.

Scones are at their best eaten the day they are baked. However, if frozen upon cooling, they can be defrosted satisfactorily in a microwave oven using 50 per cent power. Use a light hand when making scones. They are split with a fork and eaten with butter or clotted cream and jam. I developed the following recipe with the help of a dear English mum during her visit to the States when we held a tea class together.

Balmoral Shortbread

2   **teaspoons unsalted butter to grease pans**

3   **cups all-purpose flour**

8   **ounces unsalted butter, softened**

½   **cup granulated sugar**

2   **tablespoons granulated sugar for sprinkling**

❉ Preheat oven to 325 degrees F. Butter 2 (8-inch) square non-stick pans. Sift flour into large mixing bowl.

❉ Cut the butter into 32 equal pieces. Rub the butter into the flour. Add the sugar, mixing well. Turn out onto floured work surface and knead until smooth.

❉ Press mixture evenly into prepared pans. With a tined fork, prick all over in a pattern. Bake for 20 minutes. Reduce heat to 300 degrees F. and bake for 15 to 20 minutes more or until light golden color. Remove from oven. Cut into 1 x 2-inch fingers while still warm. Sprinkle each pan with 1 tablespoon of granulated sugar. Let cool in the pans set on a wire rack. Once cooled, they can be frozen.

Yields: 64 shortbread.

Grace Falvey of Hampton Manor, England sent this treat to me on a Christmas card. She says it came from the recipe files of Queen Victoria's chef at Balmoral Castle.

Maids of Honour Tarts

Pastry:

1⅔   cups unbleached all-purpose
        flour

¼   teaspoon salt

1   tablespoon granulated sugar

4   ounces unsalted butter, frozen

1   large egg

4 to 5 tablespoons ice water

❀ Place flour, salt and sugar in food processor with steel blade and process to blend. Cut butter into 16 equal pieces and scatter over the flour. Process until butter is size of peas.

❀ Beat egg with ice water. With processor running, pour the mixture down the feed tube. Process just to bring together. Test mixture to feel if it is moist enough to stick together. A bit more ice water may be needed. Turn dough out on plastic wrap and use your hands to form a flat disk. Refrigerate 30 minutes.

❀ On a lightly floured surface, roll pastry out thinly with floured rolling pin. Lift and rotate dough a quarter turn, dusting with flour. Use a 1½-inch fluted pastry cutter and cut pastry rounds. Line mini-muffin pans with pastry. Prick bottoms of tarts with tines of a fork. Chill.

❀ Preheat oven to 350 degrees F.

Filling:

2	**large eggs**
½	**cup granulated sugar**
2	**tablespoons unsalted butter**
2	**tablespoons all-purpose flour**
½	**cup blanched ground almonds**
1	**teaspoon grated lemon peel**
1	**teaspoon brandy**
2	**tablespoons dried currants**
¼	**cup confectioners' sugar**

❀ In food processor bowl, place all ingredients but the currants and confectioners' sugar. Process until smooth.

❀ Spoon a tablespoon of the filling into each tart and top with currants. Bake for 15 minutes or until golden. Remove from oven. Turn tarts out, using a paring knife to facilitate their removal from the muffin tins, onto a wire rack to cool. Dust with confectioners' sugar.

Yields: 4 dozen tarts.

This sweet was a favorite of Anne Boleyn and is reputed to have been given its name by Henry VIII. They are a specialty served in tea rooms surrounding Hampton Court Palace. I have modernized the filling, thanks to the food processor, from the British one which calls for curdling raw milk with rennet.

Seed Cake

1	teaspoon unsalted butter to grease pan
2	cups all-purpose flour
2	teaspoons baking powder
¼	teaspoon salt
8	ounces unsalted butter, softened
1½	cups granulated sugar
4	large eggs
1	teaspoon rose water or vanilla extract
2	tablespoons caraway seeds

> *This is like a pound cake flavored with caraway seeds. The English have been baking this cake since Shakespeare's time and the original caraway cake came from a convent. If you do not like caraway seeds, try substituting poppyseeds. For a birthday tea, I wrapped the outside perimeter with a festive cotton ribbon.*

❀ Preheat oven to 350 degrees F. Butter an 8-inch deep round cake pan. Line the bottom with buttered parchment paper. Sift flour, baking powder and salt onto waxed paper and set aside.

❀ With electric mixer, cream butter. Add sugar slowly and cream until mixture is light and fluffy. Add eggs, one at a time, beating well at medium speed. Add the rose water and cream the mixture 2 minutes.

❀ Add the flour mixture with the caraway seeds and beat to combine. Spread batter in cake pan and bake 1 hour, or until cake is golden and shrinks from sides of pan. Remove from oven and cool in pan for 5 minutes.

❀ Turn out on a wire rack, peel off the parchment paper and cool completely.

Yields: 20 slices.

Note: Cake may also be baked in a 2 pound loaf pan or a Bundt pan for a prettier presentation.

Sponge Sandwich Cake

1	teaspoon unsalted butter to grease pan
3	large eggs
½	cup granulated sugar
¾	cup all-purpose flour
	Pinch of salt
	Fresh raspberries or strawberries
½	cup heavy cream, whipped
	Confectioners' sugar

❀ Preheat oven to 350 degrees F. Butter an 8-inch cake pan and line with buttered parchment paper. Sprinkle with granulated sugar.

❀ In mixing bowl, beat eggs until light and pale before gradually adding the sugar. Beat until mousse-like and triple in volume. Sift flour with salt 3 times onto waxed paper. When eggs and sugar are light and fluffy, sift in the flour in 3 folds. Fold gently. Turn into cake pan and bake 25 to 30 minutes, until golden and springy. Turn out on to a cooling rack; remove parchment paper. Cover with a tea towel.

❀ When cool, split cake in half horizontally with serrated knife. Spread bottom layer with whipped cream and berries. Place top on bottom layer and sprinkle with confectioners' sugar.

Yields: 10 slices.

A cake that is meant to absorb luscious berry juices. The original recipe used equal amounts of eggs, sugar and flour. This is the sponge used in trifles.

Boxing Day

Boxing day is a traditional English custom that takes place the day after Christmas. The tradesmen, who had to work on Christmas, visited their customers with a wooden box expecting to receive a few pence as a thank you for their services. Our British neighbors celebrated with a party that started at noon with typical British food and spirits. We have continued to have an annual Boxing Day party since our return to the States.

Boxing Day Buffet

Onion Pie

Tea Flavored Gravlax

Stilton Walnut Spread

Massaman Curry over Rice

English Trifle

Barm Brack Tea Cake

Macaroon Mincemeat Tarts

Christmas Pudding

Spiced Tea Punch (page 181)

Sherry and Ales

Onion Pie

Pastry:

1⅔   **cups unbleached all-purpose flour**

4   **ounces unsalted butter, very cold**

      Pinch of salt

5 to 6 tablespoons ice water

This recipe is from my first cooking class in Normandy where I was the only American among fifty British students. The onions and the pastry may be prepared two weeks in advance and frozen. If you wish to bake the pie, be sure to cool it completely before wrapping tightly for the freezer. Defrost the day before the party and freshen it by placing in a 350 degree F. oven for 10 minutes.

Onion Filling:

3   **medium-size sweet onions, peeled, sliced thinly**

2   **tablespoons heavy cream**

3   **large eggs**

½   **teaspoon salt**

      Freshly ground white pepper

      Freshly ground nutmeg

❀ Sift flour with salt into mixing bowl. Cut butter into 8 equal pieces. Use your fingertips or a pastry blender and rub in the butter until mixture is like oatmeal. Sprinkle over the water and mix lightly with a wooden spoon. Gather into a ball, flatten into a disc and wrap in plastic wrap. Refrigerate 1 hour.

❀ Preheat oven to 425 degrees F. Roll pastry on floured surface to a ⅛-inch thickness. Butter a 12-inch quiche pan with a removable bottom. Line the pan with the pastry, building up the sides. Chill 15 minutes.

❀ Prick bottom of pastry evenly with a fork. Bake with a blind of pie weights or beans for 7 minutes. Remove the blind and bake for 3 more minutes. Pastry is ready for filling.

❀ Preheat oven to 375 degrees F. Foam the butter in a large sauté pan and sauté the onions until soft.

❀ Whisk the cream with the eggs and seasonings. Pour into the pre-baked pastry-lined pan. Bake for 30 to 35 minutes, until golden.

❀ Remove pie from oven. May be served warm or at room temperature.

Yields: 12 servings.

Tea Flavored Gravlax

2 pounds fresh salmon fillet with skin

¼ cup sugar

2 tablespoons coarse sea salt

2 tablespoons Rose Pouchong tea

Extra-thin dark sandwich bread

Unsalted butter, softened

1 burpless cucumber, peeled, diced

Salt and freshly ground white pepper

❀ Remove any bones from the salmon with needle-nose pliers. If you are able to purchase the tail end of the salmon, there will be few, if any bones to remove. Combine the sugar and salt and rub the mixture on both sides of the salmon. Distribute the tea leaves evenly on the fleshy side of the salmon.

❀ Place a large piece of plastic wrap on top of a larger piece of aluminum foil. Lay 1 fillet, skin side down, on the plastic wrap and lay the other fillet on top with the skin side up. Wrap well in the plastic wrap and enclose the salmon packet in the foil. Place in a glass dish, cover with plastic wrap and refrigerate for 24 hours.

❀ Unwrap the salmon, drain off the accumulated juices. Turn the salmon upside down and rewrap tightly. Place weights on the salmon so it will compact and be easier to slice. Put the fish back in the refrigerator for another 24 hours. Unwrap the salmon fillets and scrape the tea leaves off. Discard the liquid.

❀ Butter the dark bread. Peel and dice the cucumber. Season with salt and freshly ground white pepper.

❀ Slice the salmon with a salmon slicing knife or a knife that has a scalloped edge. Slice from the tail at a right angle into very thin slices. Place the slices on the dark buttered bread and garnish with the diced cucumber. Place on serving platter.

❀ I have a salmon-shaped serving board that I place the cured salmon on and serve it as needed with the buttered bread and cucumber garnish on the side.

Yields: 36 appetizers.

Note: For additional flavor, use vanilla flavored sugar as vanilla and tea marry very well.

Instead of serving costly Scottish smoked salmon, I created this alternative dish which has received raves from my Boxing Day guests. It may be prepared three days in advance or even two weeks ahead and frozen. However, the texture changes when frozen and the slices are not quite as translucent.

Stilton Walnut Spread

½ **cup walnuts pieces, toasted at 350 degrees F. until golden**

6 **ounces Stilton cheese, softened**

3 **ounces cream cheese, softened**

2 **tablespoons heavy cream**

   English water biscuits (crackers)

1 **tablespoon port or sherry**

   Pears and apples

❀ With metal blade in food processor, process Stilton and cream cheese until smooth. Add the cream, port and ¼ cup of walnuts. Turn out into a bowl lined with plastic wrap. Cover and refrigerate.

❀ Unmold and garnish with remaining chopped walnuts. Serve with water biscuits surrounded by sliced pears and apples.

Yields: 1 ½ cups spread.

Note: For a large party, I have tripled this recipe and piped a portion on a 7-inch cake stand.

Stilton is the king of British cheeses. Search for one of the available farmhouse brands. This spread may be prepared 7 days in advance and refrigerated.

Massaman Curry

4	cloves garlic
½	teaspoon cayenne pepper
2	tablespoons ground coriander
2	teaspoons ground cumin
½	teaspoon ground fennel
½	teaspoon ground cloves
1	teaspoon ground ginger
½	teaspoon ground cinnamon
1	teaspoon shrimp paste (available in Oriental markets)
1	teaspoon chopped gingerroot
3	tablespoons peanut oil
1	large onion, chopped
2	pounds boneless beef chuck, cut into small cubes
3	tablespoons fish sauce (available in Oriental markets)
¾	cup thick coconut milk
2	tablespoons lime juice
2	teaspoons brown sugar
2	tablespoons tamarind water

✤ Combine the garlic, spices, shrimp paste and gingerroot in an electric blender and blend until smooth. In large saucepan, heat the oil and fry the spices and onion until it darkens and separates. Add the cubed meat and cook for 5 minutes. Add the fish sauce and the coconut milk. Simmer for 35 to 40 minutes or until beef is tender.

✤ Add the lime juice, brown sugar, tamarind water; simmer for 5 minutes. Serve with cooked long grain rice and condiments: Chutney, salted peanuts, diced bananas, grated coconut, chopped scallions, sliced hard-cooked eggs.

Yields: 10 servings.

The first Boxing Day party I attended in my British neighbor's home, I was served this delicious curry. Failing to get the recipe, I later had a student in my cooking classes who shared her recipe from her Thai cook in Bangkok. It freezes beautifully.

English Trifle

Cake:

1	recipe Sponge Sandwich Cake (page 59)
½	cup raspberry jam
4	ounces cream sherry
6 to 8	pear halves, canned or poached
1	cup seedless red grapes, sliced in half
½	cup almonds, toasted, finely chopped
1	cup heavy cream

Custard:

1	cup heavy cream
2	cups half-and-half cream
1	vanilla bean
4	large eggs
4	egg yolks
¾	cup granulated sugar
1	tablespoon cornstarch

✤ Split the sponge cake in half with a serrated knife and spread each half with the jam. Sandwich the halves together and cut into 1-inch squares. Arrange the cake squares in the bottom of a glass trifle bowl that should be about 12 inches in diameter and about 3 inches deep. Sprinkle the cake with the sherry and some of the pear liquid. Top with the pears.

✤ For the custard, bring the cream and the half-and-half to the boil with the vanilla bean in a large heavy pan. Remove from the heat. In mixing bowl, whisk the eggs and egg yolks with the sugar and cornstarch until light in color. Remove the vanilla bean from the cream mixture. Gradually add half of the hot cream to the whisked eggs to temper the eggs. Return the mixture to the pan and stir over a low heat until it coats the back of a wooden spoon. Remove from the heat and strain into a bowl. Sprinkle with a bit of granulated sugar or place a lightly buttered piece of plastic wrap over the custard to prevent a skin from forming. Cool before pouring over the cake.

✤ Pour custard over the cake and pears slowly. Place grape halves around the outside perimeter of the trifle.

✤ Whip the cup of cream in a chilled bowl until stiff enough to pipe. Put whipped cream into a pastry bag fitted with a ½-inch star tube. Pipe rosettes around the custard. Sprinkle with the toasted almonds. Refrigerate until serving.

Yields: 12 servings.

Note: The sponge cake may be baked one month in advance and frozen. The trifle can be assembled a day in advance but the whipping cream on the top is to be added the day of the party.

Try this recipe in the summer when fresh berries are available and use fresh peaches in place of the canned pears. My British neighbor told me to always use as much cream as I could afford in the custard.

Barm Brack Tea Cake

1   **pound mixed candied fruit (orange peel, currants, sultanas)**

1¼   **cups strong cold tea**

1   **cup dark brown sugar**

❁ Mix the above in a bowl, cover and leave overnight to plump the fruit.

1   **tablespoon unsalted butter and**

2   **tablespoons flour for the baking pan**

1   **large egg, beaten**

1   **tablespoon orange marmalade**

2   **cups all-purpose flour**

2½   **teaspoons baking powder**

1   **teaspoon ground allspice**

❁ Preheat oven to 350 degrees F. Butter, flour and line bottom with parchment paper, a 9 x 5 x 1½-inch loaf pan or a 7-inch round cake pan. Beat egg and marmalade into the fruit. Sift flour, baking powder and allspice into the mixture and mix with a wooden spoon just to blend. Bake for 1½ hours or until a wooden toothpick inserted in the middle of the cake is clean. If cake is brown and not yet done, place a sheet of foil loosely over the top to prevent over-browning. Remove from oven and cool 10 minutes before turning out of the pan onto a wire rack to cool.

Yields: 20 servings.

I tasted this wonderful tea cake with a cuppa brewed over a GAZ stove on the parking lot at Bruges in Belgium with Ethel Peskett and her daughter. The cake had been riding around in a cake tin in the boot of their car for two weeks but was wonderfully moist despite its travels. I often take it along on trips abroad to nibble on when I am jet lagged. I contributed this recipe to the **James Beard Celebration Cookbook.**

Macaroon Mincemeat Tarts

Tart Pastry:

1⅔	cups unbleached all-purpose flour
	Pinch salt
1	tablespoon granulated sugar
4	ounces unsalted butter, frozen
1	large egg
¼	cup ice water

Filling:

½	cup mincemeat
2	large egg whites
¼	cup granulated sugar
¼	cup ground almonds
¼	cup flaked almonds
3	candied cherries, cut into quarters

❈ Place flour, salt and sugar into work bowl of food processor. Cut butter into 8 equal pieces and add to bowl. Pulse with quick on/off. Beat egg with ice water and add to work bowl through feed tube with processor running. Process just to bring together. Remove and wrap pastry in plastic wrap and refrigerate 30 minutes. Freeze for 1 month in freezer plastic bag.

❈ Roll out the pastry on floured surface and with 3-inch fluted cutter; stamp out 12 circles. Line 12 muffin pans with pastry rounds.

❈ Preheat oven to 375 degrees F. Divide the mincemeat equally between the tarts. Whisk the egg whites until stiff. Fold in the sugar and ground almonds. Pile the mixture on top of the mincemeat and sprinkle with the flaked almonds. Top with a cherry quarter. Bake 15 to 20 minutes or until golden brown.

Yields: 12 tarts.

Christmas Pudding

Pudding:

⅔	cup dried currants
1⅓	cups sultanas
1⅓	cups raisins
¼	cup chopped mixed candied peel
¼	cup chopped candied cherries
1	lemon, zest and juice
3	tablespoons brandy
½	cup brewed tea
1	cup self-rising flour
1	teaspoon ground allspice
½	teaspoon grated nutmeg
½	teaspoon ground cinnamon
	Pinch of salt
4	ounces beef suet, very cold
1½	cups fresh white bread crumbs
4	large eggs
1	cup brown sugar
1	tablespoon unsalted butter, softened

❈ Place first 5 ingredients along with lemon rind and juice in large mixing bowl and pour on the brandy and tea. Cover and leave overnight to plump the fruit. Sift flour, spices and salt together over the dried fruit. Shred the suet (freezing makes it easier to shred) in food processor and add to mixture along with the bread crumbs. Beat eggs and sugar together until light in color and add to mixture. If pudding appears to be stiff, add a bit of milk or ale to achieve a medium soft texture. Cover and refrigerate 12 hours to mellow.

❈ Butter a 3-pint pudding mold or 3 (1-pint) pudding bowls. Fill molds ¾ full with the mixture. Cover with buttered rounds of parchment paper with a pleat in the middle for expansion. Cover with foil and tie with a string.

❈ Place molds in steamer or large roaster. Pour boiling water ⅓ up sides of mold. Cover pan and steam for 6 hours, replenishing water as it boils away. Remove from pan, cool, remove all coverings and cover with fresh foil.

❈ Refrigerate at least 3 weeks before serving. May be kept in freezer properly wrapped for 1 year.

❈ To serve, re-steam for 2 hours and unmold on heatproof serving platter. Flame with brandy warmed in a soup ladle. Serve with Hard Sauce.

Hard Sauce:

¼   **cup unsalted butter**

1   **cup confectioners' sugar**

3   **tablespoons brandy**

 Combine the above in mixing bowl and beat with an electric mixer until smooth. Refrigerate to harden.

Yields: 18 servings.

While living on Pollards Hill in South London, I became a fan of Christmas or English Plum Pudding. I bought my first one from the local bakery and decided to develop a recipe once I started teaching in the United States. My students loved it.

Queen Victoria Birthday Tea

One of the most popular classes among my students has been the one where we celebrate the birthday of Queen Vicky on May 24. She often baked the sweets for her Prince Consort Albert. The longer she ruled, the greater she grew in girth.

Queen Victoria Birthday Tea

Potted Stilton Cheese

Koulibiac of Salmon

Sausage Rolls

Compote of Spiced Pears

Treacle Tart

Dundee Cake

Victoria Sponge Cake

Cream Sherry

Queen Mothers Blend

Potted Stilton Cheese

8	**ounces Stilton cheese, softened**
4	**ounces unsalted butter, softened**
2	**tablespoons port or sherry**
	Walnut halves for garnish

 In bowl of food processor, combine the cheese and butter to blend. Stir in the port. Place in a serving bowl and decorate with walnut halves. If you wish to do this a week ahead, omit the walnut halves and cover the mixture with a layer of clarified butter.

 Serve with English cream crackers and walnuts.

Yields: 2 cups.

This spread may also be used as a sandwich filling and topped with watercress sprigs for an open-faced sandwich.

Koulibiac of Salmon

Rich Short Crust Pastry:

3	cups unbleached all-purpose flour
½	teaspoon salt
6	ounces unsalted butter
2	large egg yolks
½	cup ice water
1	egg, beaten

Fish Filling:

2	pounds fresh salmon, skinned, deboned
½	cup rice, cooked, cooled
4	large eggs, hard-cooked, peeled, sliced
2	tablespoons chopped fresh dill
2	tablespoons unsalted butter, melted
	Salt and freshly ground white pepper
¼	teaspoon mace
1	egg, beaten
1	cup sour cream
1	tablespoon chopped fresh dill

❀ In large mixing bowl, mix flour and salt. Cut butter into 6 equal pieces and using a pastry blender, cut into the flour. Blend until mixture is size of large peas. Whisk egg yolks with ½ cup of ice water and stir into mixture. Mix to bring together and the dough may require a bit more of the ice water. Knead lightly and wrap in plastic wrap. Refrigerate for 30 minutes.

❀ Make pastry and chill for 30 minutes. Slice salmon and chop trimmings. Mix the trimmings with the rice, chopped dill, 1 tablespoon of the melted butter, salt, pepper and mace.

❀ Preheat oven to 425 degrees F. On floured surface, roll out two-thirds of the pastry; reserve one-third for the top. Line a 10-inch springform pan with the pastry. Put a layer of the rice mixture on the pastry followed by a layer of the salmon slices and a layer of the sliced eggs. Repeat, ending with the rice on top. Pour on the melted butter.

❀ Roll out the pastry top and place on the pie, pressing around the edges and sealing with water. Make steam hole in the middle of the pastry top and prick with a fork. Brush with the beaten egg and prick with a fork. Make a rose from the pastry trimmings and place around the steam hole. Brush with the egg wash. Bake for 25 minutes. Reduce oven to 400 degrees F. and bake for 15 to 20 more minutes, until golden.

✤ Remove to cooling rack; cool 15 minutes. Serve with sour cream mixed with fresh dill.

Yields: 10 servings.

My French cooking teacher in London taught this as an easier way to make this dish.

Sausage Rolls

½ **pound puff pastry (store bought is fine)**

1 **pound seasoned pork sausage**

1 **egg, beaten with 1 teaspoon water**

❋ Cut chilled pastry in 2 pieces. Roll into lengthwise strips. Trim to 5-inch width. Divide sausage in half and shape into long rope to fit pastry. Place sausage roll on pastry. Moisten pastry with water and fold over to enclose filling. Then press and seal.

❋ Cut each roll crosswise in 2-inch rolls; cut 2 small diagonal slits on top of each roll. Place seam side down on baking tray lined with parchment paper. Refrigerate 10 minutes and preheat oven to 400 degrees F.

❋ Brush rolls with egg wash. Bake about 20 to 25 minutes or until golden brown. Serve warm.

Yields: 24 sausage rolls.

A cooking student married to an Englishman dared me to make a decent sausage roll rather than the tough ones found in the train stations of Great Britain. Her mate heartily approved the result.

Compote of Spiced Pears

1	cup granulated sugar
1	cup water
1	stick of cinnamon
¼	teaspoon ground ginger
1	lemon, zest and juice
6	firm pears (like Bosc), peeled and cored

In large saucepan, bring sugar and water to a boil with the cinnamon, ginger, lemon zest and juice. Place pears, skin-side down and cover with parchment paper and a dinner plate. Simmer until pears are tender, about 30 to 40 minutes; depends on the ripeness of the pears. Remove pears to a serving dish and reduce the syrup to thicken by boiling. Remove cinnamon and pour syrup over pears. Cool.

Yields: 12 servings.

In the back garden of my home in London, I had two varieties of pear trees that bore a lot of fruit. I created this recipe to serve with roasted duck but it pairs well with the salmon dish.

Treacle Tart

Rich Short-Crust Pastry (page 74)

8   ounces Golden Syrup
        (Lyons is the British brand)

1½   slices white bread, processed to crumbs

1   tablespoon lime juice

1   teaspoon lime zest

¾   teaspoon fresh gingerroot, grated finely

1   large egg

1   large egg yolk

1   cup heavy cream

Preheat oven to 425 degrees F. Roll out pastry thinly on lightly floured surface and line tart pan, trimming excess dough. Chill.

In bowl, mix syrup, bread crumbs, lime juice, zest, and grated gingerroot together. Whisk egg and egg yolk together and combine with previous mixture. Pour into pastry crust. Bake for 5 minutes; turn oven down to 350 degrees F. Bake for 30 more minutes or until top is nicely browned. Serve warm with cream poured over it.

Yields: 10 slices.

The cooking student married to the British nobleman brought this hand-written recipe from her mother-in-law for me to try. We found it to be the best treacle tart we ever tasted.

Dundee Cake

2	ounces mixed citrus peel (lemon and orange)
8	ounces golden raisins
8	ounces seedless raisins
¼	cup candied cherries
¼	cup Scotch whiskey
6	ounces unsalted butter, softened, plus 1 teaspoon to grease pan
2½	cups all-purpose flour
2	teaspoons baking powder
½	teaspoon salt
1	teaspoon ground allspice
2	tablespoons ground almonds
⅔	cup granulated sugar
5	large eggs
	Whole blanched almonds for decoration
	Whole candied cherries for decoration, cut in half

A traditional Scottish fruity cake that would have graced the birthday menu.

❀ In food processor, chop citrus peel, raisins and cherries. Put fruit in a large bowl and sprinkle with the whiskey. Let stand, covered with plastic wrap, overnight.

❀ Butter a 10-inch round deep cake pan and line it with double parchment paper, also buttered. Preheat oven to 325 degrees F.

❀ Sift flour, baking powder, salt and allspice onto waxed paper; add ground almonds. Place softened butter in mixer bowl and cream with paddle. Add sugar slowly, beating to a creamy texture. Add the eggs, one at a time, beating well after each addition. Add the flour, a third at a time, and mix well. Fold in the plumped fruit. Turn out into prepared cake pan and decorate with almonds. Bake for 2 hours, or until done when a skewer is inserted into the center and comes out clean.

❀ After 1 hour, if the cake is becoming too brown, cover the top loosely with foil. When done remove from oven, cover with a tea towel and leave to cool in pan for moistness. To remove from pan, warm in the oven and turn out on waxed paper. Place upright on cooling rack to cool. Decorate with whole almonds and cherry halves. Wrap in foil and let flavors mature for 1 week prior to serving.

Yields: 16 servings.

Victoria Sponge Cake

1   **cup unsalted butter, softened**

1   **cup granulated sugar**

4   **large eggs**

1¾   **cups self-rising flour**

2   **tablespoons warm water**

⅓   **cup raspberry jam**

1   **tablespoon confectioners' sugar**

❀ Preheat oven to 350 degrees F. Butter and sugar 2 (8-inch) round cake pans whose bottoms have been lined with parchment paper.

❀ In mixing bowl of electric mixer, cream the butter until light. Add the sugar gradually and continue to cream until fluffy. Add eggs one at a time, beating well after each addition. Lightly fold in sifted flour a third at a time along with the water. Divide the batter between the prepared pans.

❀ Bake for 25 to 30 minutes, until golden and springy to the touch. Cool in pans for 5 minutes before turning out onto cooling wire rack. Remove the parchment paper and cool completely.

❀ Sandwich together with the raspberry jam and dust top with sifted confectioners' sugar.

Yields: 10 slices.

Variation: Whipped cream rosettes may be piped on top of cake and each rosette topped with a fresh raspberry.

> *Named for the Queen, this was reputed to be her favorite cake. Equal amounts of butter, flour and eggs were the measurement in Queen Victoria's day.*

New Ways with Tea

Floral Tea

"Gather ye rosebuds while ye may,
Old Time is still a-flying:
And this same flower that smiles to-day,
Tomorrow will be dying."

Robert Herrick 1591-1674

As a lover of old English roses, I have several varieties in my garden that I often use in recipes for my tea classes. The English have used rose water since Elizabethan times and primroses were very popular in the Victorian era. With the current use of edible flowers and herbs, I created a menu for a floral tea that was a hit with my students. You must be careful about the use of chemicals in your garden if you wish to safely eat flowers and herbs, which may be used to flavor jams and jellies, in sandwiches, cordials, butters, breads, salads, cakes, ice cream, teas and punches to name a few. Be certain they are non-toxic and pesticide-free.

Floral Tea

Nasturtium Rounds

Marigold Mint Egg Salad Fingers

Cucumber Sandwiches with Mint Butter

Dilled Scones with Smoked Salmon

Raspberry Cream Filo Tarts

Scottish Rose Geranium Cake

Lavender Ice Cream

Rose Petal Champagne Punch (page 176)

Black Currant Tea

Nasturtium Rounds

6   **slices extra-thin white bread**

6   **tablespoons unsalted butter, softened**

24   **nasturtium blossoms**

Spread the bread slices thinly with butter on one side. Using a 1½-inch fluted cutter, stamp out 4 rounds per slice. Top with finely chopped nasturtium petals pressing so they adhere to the butter. Arrange on clear glass tray and garnish with whole blossoms.

Yields: 24 rounds.

The English love of nasturtiums developed after the flower was brought to them from the New World. They use it in salads and sandwiches where it imparts a peppery taste similar to watercress.

Marigold Mint Egg Salad Fingers

4   **hard-cooked eggs, peeled and chopped finely**

2   **tablespoons mayonnaise**

     Salt and freshly ground white pepper, to taste

1   **tablespoon marigold mint leaves, chopped fine**

4   **ounces unsalted butter, softened**

12   **slices extra-thin whole wheat bread**

12   **edible marigold mint blossoms**

In a mixing bowl combine eggs with mayonnaise and season with salt and pepper. In another bowl add the marigold mint leaves to the softened butter. Spread the slices of bread with the mint butter and fill with the egg salad. Remove petals from 6 of the marigold blossoms and sprinkle each sandwich filling with a bit of petals. Sandwich bread slices together and decrust. Slice into 4 fingers. Place on sandwich tray and garnish with remaining marigold mint blossoms.

Yields: 24 fingers.

Marigold mint is an herb used in Southwest cooking and it has a very pronounced flavor similar to tarragon. The blossoms may be used to spark up a mixed green salad.

Cucumber Sandwiches with Mint Butter

4	ounces unsalted butter, softened
¼	cup mint (lemon or spearmint), finely chopped
12	slices extra-thin white sandwich bread
	Burpless English cucumber, thinly sliced

In bowl cream butter until soft and fluffy; add chopped mint. Spread the bread slices with a thin layer of mint butter. Arrange 4 to 5 slices of cucumber on one slice of bread; top with other buttered slice. Decrust bread and cut into triangles.

Yields: 24 triangles.

The English cucumber sandwich can be a delicious treat if properly prepared. The use of mint butter provides a refreshing base for the cucumber. Borage is another herb that may be used in place of the mint.

Dilled Scones with Smoked Salmon

4	cups all-purpose unbleached flour
5	teaspoons baking powder
1	teaspoon salt
2	tablespoons fresh dill weed, chopped
4	ounces unsalted butter, cut into 8 equal pieces
1	egg
1	cup milk plus 1 tablespoon, divided use
1	cup sour cream
4	ounces smoked salmon, thinly sliced into curls
	Fresh dill for garnish

❧ Preheat oven to 425 degrees F. In a large mixing bowl sift flour with salt and baking powder. Sprinkle in chopped dill. Cut in the butter. Beat egg with the cup of milk and mix in well in center of flour mixture. Mix until combined. Bring mixture together and turn out on floured surface. Pat out to ¾-inch thickness and cut into 1⅞-inch rounds. Place on greased baking sheet and paint tops with the 1 tablespoon of milk. Bake for 10 minutes.

❧ Remove from oven and place scones on wire rack to cool. Split and spread with sour cream. Top with smoked salmon curls and fresh dill sprigs.

Yields: 40 halves.

I was looking for a different way to present smoked salmon other than in a sandwich when the idea occurred to me to produce a savory dilled scone. This recipe makes one forget all about scones with cream.

Raspberry Cream Filo Tea Tarts

6	sheets filo pastry dough
4	ounces unsalted butter, melted
3	ounces cream cheese, softened
¼	cup sour cream
2	tablespoons sugar
1	teaspoon lemon zest
1	4-ounce box fresh raspberries, divided use
2	large cabbage roses with edible petals, white base removed

❀ Unfold filo pastry sheets. Place one sheet on pastry surface and paint pastry sheet with melted butter. Top with remaining pastry sheets, painting each sheet with butter including top sheet. Using a 2¼-inch round fluted cutter, cut out pastry rounds. Line mini-muffin pans with the pastry rounds, buttered side down. Prick bottoms with a fork and freeze 10 minutes.

❀ Preheat oven to 375 degrees F. Bake tart rounds on baking trays for 5 minutes. Remove from oven and press any bubbles out with flat side of a teaspoon. Return to oven for 5 minutes or until golden. Turn tarts out on wire rack to cool.

❀ In blender combine cream cheese with sour cream, sugar and lemon zest blending until smooth. Add half of berries and blend.

❀ To serve: Use a pastry bag fitted with ½-inch plain tip and pipe the raspberry cream filling into each tart. Top with fresh raspberry in center of filling and garnish with two rose petals.

Yields: 30 tea tarts.

This is a quick recipe to execute, as there is no pastry to be made. The filo cups may be made in advance and kept in an airtight container until you fill them shortly before serving.

Scottish Rose Geranium Cake

6-8 **rose geranium leaves, well washed and dried, pesticide free**

8 **ounces unsalted butter, softened**

⅔ **cup dark brown sugar**

1 **tablespoon vanilla extract**

3 **extra-large eggs, separated**

1½ **cups all-purpose flour**

1½ **teaspoons baking soda**

¼ **teaspoon salt**

1 **cup half-and-half**

3 **tablespoons granulated sugar**

½ **cup raisins, lightly floured**

½ **cup lightly toasted walnuts, chopped**

2 **tablespoons confectioners' sugar**
  Rose geranium leaves for garnish

❦ Preheat oven to 350 degrees F. Butter a 10-inch tube pan and line bottom with parchment paper. Layer bottom of pan with fresh rose geranium leaves.

❦ In mixing bowl cream butter, brown sugar and vanilla until light. Beat in egg yolks. Sift flour, baking soda and salt together. Mix into creamed cake mixture alternating with the half-and-half.

❦ Beat egg whites to soft peaks and gradually add granulated sugar. Fold part into the cake batter. Add the raisins and walnuts; fold in remaining egg whites. Pour into tube pan and bake for 45 to 60 minutes. Cool 5 minutes and turn out onto wire rack to cool. Dust with confectioners' sugar. Display on your prettiest cake stand and garnish with fresh rose geranium leaves. Lavender Ice Cream may be served on the side.

Yields: 20 slices.

A dear culinary instructor repeatedly told me about this wonderful cake her great-grandmother baked from a recipe she brought over from Scotland. When she read the ingredients to me there were no ingredient amounts. Undaunted, we found the rose geranium plant and I developed the following cake which my friend says is almost as she remembers the taste. The rose geranium flavor can be intensified if you bury half a dozen of the leaves in the sugar for a week prior to baking the cake.

Lavender Ice Cream

2   **cups milk**

1   **cup lavender honey**

4   **egg yolks**

1   **cup whipping cream**

❀ Bring milk to boil in saucepan: add honey, stirring well and bring back to boil. If you have fresh lavender flowers and leaves, you may infuse the milk with 2 tablespoons of them for 10 minutes and then strain the milk. The mixture will have to be sweetened with 1 cup of granulated sugar.

❀ Whisk egg yolks in small bowl and add the hot milk. Return to medium heat and cook until mixture coats a wooden spoon. Strain into bowl, add cream and chill. Freeze in ice cream machine for 30 minutes or until firm.

Yields: 1 quart.

On a trip to Provence I discovered this addictive lemony tasting treat. The only difficult part of the recipe is finding the lavender honey but it is becoming more readily available.

Corporate Tea

Tea is rapidly replacing the power breakfast as the time slot for accomplishing business. Taking a break at 4pm for tea eases tension, slows people down, and allows them time to think. One can have a private conversation, as cocktail places are often noisy and poorly lit. If served in the office, be sure the cups and saucers are porcelain and the teaspoons may be silver-plated but the sugar tongs and lemon fork should be silver.

Corporate tea parties are being given in private hotel rooms where people are seated with fine china and cloth napkins with the tea served from large samovars.

Corporate Tea Menu

Open-Faced Sandwiches of Sliced Beef

Cheese Pâté on Thin Whole Wheat Bread

Shrimp Halves on Thin Pumpernickel Bread

Almond Macaroons

Chocolate Shortbread

Keemun

Open-Faced Sandwiches of Sliced Beef

4   **ounces unsalted butter, softened**

1   **tablespoon prepared horseradish**

8   **slices extra-thin white bread**

4   **ounces thinly sliced rare roast beef**

16   **sprigs of fresh watercress**

In bowl combine butter and horseradish. Spread on bread. Decrust bread; cut in half diagonally. Divide beef slices into 16 equal pieces. Top each diagonal slice of bread with a roast beef curl. Garnish with the watercress sprigs.

Yields: 16 open-faced sandwiches.

Purchase rare roast beef from a gourmet deli for a smashing sandwich.

Cheese Pâté on Thin Whole Wheat Bread

8   **ounces English Cheddar cheese, grated**

8   **ounces Double Gloucester cheese, grated**

3   **ounces cream cheese, softened**

4   **pickled onions, chopped**

2   **tablespoons unsalted butter, softened**

1   **teaspoon freshly ground white pepper**

1   **bunch fresh chives, finely chopped**

8   **slices extra-thin whole wheat bread**

8   **radishes, thinly sliced**

❀ In a food processor, combine the cheeses, onions, butter and pepper. Process to smooth consistency.

❀ Place on plastic wrap and shape into a smooth round cylinder 1-inch in diameter. Refrigerate to firm up. Unwrap and coat evenly with the chives. Rewrap and refrigerate.

❀ Decrust bread slices 2 at a time. Slice into 4 triangles and top with a slice of the cheese pâté. Garnish with a radish slice.

Yields: 32 triangles.

This is a variation on a Ploughman's pub lunch in England.

Shrimp Halves on Thin Pumpernickel Bread

3	ounces cream cheese, softened
3	ounces unsalted butter, softened
¼	cup finely chopped chives
½	teaspoon salt
1	tablespoon lemon juice
16	slices thin pumpernickel bread
4	ounces medium shrimp, sliced in half lengthwise
32	parsley sprigs

In food processor combine cheese, butter, chives, salt and lemon juice. Process to smooth consistency. Spread cheese/butter mixture on the bread; decrust. Slice on diagonal into 2 triangles. Top with shrimp half. Garnish with parsley leaf.

Yields: 32 triangles.

Select premium boiled shrimp whether they are fresh or frozen.

Almond Macaroons

8   ounces almond paste
1   cup granulated sugar
2   large egg whites
¼   teaspoon almond extract
      Pinch of salt

❀ Cut pieces of a brown grocery bag to fit a cookie sheet. Preheat oven to 350 degrees F.

❀ Cut almond paste into ½-inch pieces and put into food processor bowl fitted with the steel blade. Cut up finely. Add sugar to almond mixture and process. Add 2 egg whites and almond extract. Process until whites are incorporated and no lumps remain. Whisk the third egg white with a fork and add about half of it to the almond mixture, blending well. If you like your macaroons very chewy, add all the third egg white.

❀ Fill a pastry bag, fitted with a ½-inch star tip, with the mixture. Pipe mounds about 1½ inches apart on the brown paper keeping them about ½-thick. Bake for 25 to 30 minutes.

❀ Remove macaroons attached to brown paper to a cooling rack. When cool, release macaroons by dampening the back side of the paper. Turn the macaroons over to do this; they will not be hurt by doing so. The paper will readily peel off. Let the macaroons rest on the cake rack for another half-hour to evaporate any dampness before storing. Store in an airtight tin.

Yields: 24 macaroons.

Rosie Manell taught this at The Gritti Palace in Venice where she appeared with Julia Child during the summer of 1976.

Chocolate Shortbread

2	tablespoons unsalted butter to grease pans
6	ounces semi-sweet chocolate, broken into pieces
3	cups granulated sugar
1	pound unsalted butter, softened
4	cups all-purpose flour

❁ Preheat oven to 300 degrees F. Butter 3 (8-inch) round pans and line with buttered parchment paper. In food processor bowl, chop chocolate and sugar together. With machine running, add butter 2 tablespoons at a time. Remove lid and sift in the flour. Process just until a ball forms.

❁ Divide dough into 3 pieces and pat into the pans. Cook for 50 minutes or until firm in center. Cool in pans for 5 minutes. Cut each shortbread into 8 wedges and cool. Store in airtight tins.

Yields: 24 pieces.

A truly buttery, chocolatey shortbread.

Picnic in the Vineyard

Fall Creek Vineyard is in the heart of the Hill Country, near Austin, Texas. Having been there many times during the spring when the bluebonnets are in full bloom, I have composed a selection of teas to accompany a hearty picnic spread on their patio overlooking the vineyard.

Spring Picnic

Tea-Cured Salmon in Filo Cups Topped with Basil Mayo

Ceylon Tea

Roasted and Smoked Orange Chicken

Grilled Fresh Peaches

Cabbage Slaw

Grape Muffins

Lapsang Souchong

Earl Grey Chocolate Cake

Jasmine Ice Cream

Kenya Tea

Tea-Cured Salmon in Filo Cups Topped with Basil Mayo

Use the salmon recipe in the Boxing Day Menu on page 62. The recipe for filo cups is in the Queen's Tea on page 146. For the basil mayo, add 6 chopped basil leaves to 1 cup of mayonnaise and mix well.

Roasted and Smoked Orange Chicken

1	**fat chicken, 3½ to 4 pounds**
1	**teaspoon white pepper**
1½	**teaspoons salt**
2	**navel oranges**
1	**tablespoon dark soy sauce**
1	**spring onion, washed**
¼	**cup pecan shells**
2	**teaspoons jasmine tea**
1	**tablespoon brown sugar**

On my very first trip to Hong Kong, I had a superb cooking teacher named Lucy Lo who turned out to be the Julia Child of Chinese cooking. I later returned to Hong Kong for another lesson with Lucy and she taught the class, simultaneously, in English, Chinese and Japanese. Her rendition of Orange Chicken was to roast it at very high heat that produces a very succulent bird. I added the smoking technique for additional flavor.

✤ Preheat oven to 475 degrees F. Wash chicken and dry well. Cut off wing tips (save for stock) and rub chicken with salt and pepper. Zest 1 orange and juice half of it. Mix with the soy sauce and place inside the chicken along with half an orange and the green onion.

✤ Place chicken breast side down on a rack, which has been sprayed with vegetable oil, over a roasting pan. After 20 minutes, turn chicken over so the breast is now up. Roast for 20 to 25 minutes, until leg joint is done.

✤ Line a wok with heavy-duty foil and have enough foil to come up over the edges of the wok. Scatter pecan shells, jasmine tea and sugar on bottom of wok. Place chicken on rack in wok. Cover with lid and press foil around edges of wok to contain smoke. Smoke for 10 minutes. Let cool 30 minutes.

✤ Serve with orange slices. Delicious cold as picnic fare.

Yields: 8 servings.

Note: I smoke this outdoors over my propane grill so as not to activate my smoke alarm.

Grilled Peaches

4	**large freestone peaches**
3	**tablespoons orange marmalade**

*Fredericksburg, Texas
is famous for its peaches.
As a teenager, I learned from
my mom how to preserve
this bounty.*

Bring a pot of water to the boil and put peaches in for 1 minute to facilitate peeling. Cut in half and remove pits; peel. Fill with a teaspoon of marmalade. Place peaches in a foil pan. Grill under the broiler or over an outdoor grill until soft. Serve at room temperature.

Yields: 8 servings.

Cabbage Slaw

4	**cups finely shredded cabbage**
2	**green onions, finely chopped**
½	**cup buttermilk**
½	**cup mayonnaise**
½	**teaspoon salt**
	Freshly ground black pepper

*This is my Mom's
recipe which is a favorite
of mine. She shreds the
cabbage by hand.*

After shredding cabbage, place in a plastic bag with onions and refrigerate until serving time. Mix the buttermilk, mayonnaise and salt in a measuring cup. When ready to serve, place shredded cabbage in salad bowl and pour on the buttermilk dressing. Grind pepper over cabbage to taste.

Yields: 8 servings.

Grape Muffins

1   cup seedless grapes cut in quarters

1   cup all-purpose flour

1   cup whole wheat flour

1   tablespoon baking powder

¾   teaspoon salt

      Grated rind of 1 lemon

2   large eggs, separate yolks and whites

3   tablespoons honey

1   cup sour cream

❀ Preheat oven to 375 degrees F. Line muffin pans with paper baking cups. Toss grapes with a bit of the white flour. Sift flours with baking powder and salt into mixing bowl. Add the grated lemon rind. Whisk egg yolks with honey and sour cream and add to flours. Beat egg whites in separate bowl to soft peaks. Fold into the creamy mixture.

❀ Fill muffin cups half full and bake 15 to 20 minutes. Remove from oven and place on cooling rack.

Yields: 15 large muffins or 30 mini-sized.

As the wife of a geologist, I have often been called upon to create menus for the geological wives auxiliary. One year I devised a Bride's Tea at a local hotel. The chef shared with me his recipe, which could be a tea time treat.

Earl Grey Chocolate Cake

1	tablespoon solid shortening
1	tablespoon flour
½	cup boiling water
1	tablespoon Earl Grey tea
1	cup buttermilk
2	teaspoons vanilla extract
2	cups all-purpose flour
1	teaspoon baking soda
1	cup unsweetened cocoa powder
8	ounces unsalted butter, room temperature
2	cups granulated sugar
4	large eggs

🌸 Preheat oven to 350 degrees F. Use the solid shortening and flour to grease and flour 2 (9-inch) round cake pans. Line bottoms with parchment paper.

🌸 Infuse the water with the tea for 5 minutes; strain into a large measuring cup and cool. Add the buttermilk and vanilla.

🌸 Sift the dry ingredients onto wax paper. In the mixing bowl of an electric mixer fitted with the flat paddle, cream the butter until it is light, about 1 minute. Scrap beater and sides of bowl; beat another 2 minutes. Add the eggs, one at a time. Scrap down sides of bowl and beat for 1 minute

🌸 Fold in one-fourth of the flour mixture and one-third of the tea/buttermilk and vanilla mixture. Blend and stir. Once all the ingredients are added, beat in mixer on low speed just to mix until smooth.

🌸 Pour batter into the pans and spread with a spatula. Tap pans on kitchen counter to break up any large air bubbles. Bake for 40 to 45 minutes or until the center springs back when touched lightly.

🌸 Remove from oven and cool on wire rack for 5 minutes. Run small kitchen knife around edges of cake and sides of pan to loosen. Unmold on cooling rack and peel off the parchment paper. Use cake rack to turn cake right side up. Cool before frosting.

I grew up loving my Mom's rich, moist, dark devil's food cake. When I flavored it with Earl Grey tea, it tasted even better.

Dark Chocolate Frosting

8   **ounces extra-bittersweet chocolate, finely chopped**

2   **cups whipping cream**

Instead of a confectioners' sugar frosting, I find this far easier and quicker to do. Mom agrees.

❧ Place the chopped chocolate in the bowl of an electric mixer. Put cream in a saucepan and bring to the simmer over low heat. Pour over the chocolate and whisk together to melt the chocolate. Place in refrigerator to cool, stirring every 10 minutes.

❧ Once the mixture is cold and starts to thicken, whip at low speed until it becomes lighter and whip until it thickens. Spread on cake layers.

Mom's Chocolate Frosting

1   **pound confectioners' sugar**

¾   **cup unsweetened cocoa powder**

6   **ounces unsalted butter (1½ sticks), room temperature**

1   **teaspoon vanilla extract**

½   **cup milk**

❧ Sift sugar and cocoa into mixing bowl of electric mixer. Add butter, vanilla and half the milk. Beat on low speed and add more milk slowly. Beat on medium until mixture is light and spreadable. Frost cake.

Yields: 12 servings.

You have to balance the sugar and liquid to achieve a spreadable frosting.

Jasmine Ice Cream

3	teaspoons gun powder or jasmine green tea
1¼	cups water
2	egg yolks
2	egg whites
½	cup granulated sugar
1	cup half-and-half
1	cup whipping cream

❀ Brew the tea with the water for 5 minutes. Strain 1 cup into a measuring cup. In a bowl, whisk the egg yolks and slowly add the sugar, whisking. Whisk the tea slowly into the egg yolks to temper them.

❀ In a heavy-based saucepan, bring the half-and-half and the whipping cream to the boil. Add half the mixture to the egg yolks, whisking. Return mixture to the saucepan and place over medium heat. Stir with a wooden spoon until mixture coats the back of the spoon. A puff of steam rises when this is about to occur. Do not allow the mixture to boil or it will curdle. Remove from heat and strain into ice cream maker. Cover with plastic wrap and chill.

❀ Freeze in ice cream machine until firm. You may lighten the mixture by whisking the egg whites to soft peaks and adding them to the ice cream before it is frozen.

Yields: 10 servings.

This is a delicious ice cream that may be served alongside the chocolate cake or on its own with shortbread.

Tea and Food Pairings

In Great Britain the Tea Council has worked with the Academy of Food and Wine Service to partner cheeses, afternoon tea pastries and desserts, wines and liqueurs with specific teas to enhance both the food and the wine while highlighting the specific qualities of the teas themselves. Tea is used as a digestif to clear the palate after dinner. The following chart illustrates these exciting pairings.

Tea	Afternoon Tea Pastries and Desserts	Cheese	Wine	Liqueur
Ceylon	Lemon Tart	Aged Cheddar	Dessert	Chartreuse
Kenya	Chocolate Cake	Smoked	New World Cabernet	Drambuie
Darjeeling	Cream Desserts	Cream	Zinfandel Syrah	Armagnac
Lapsang Souchong	Lemon Sorbet	Stilton	New World Chardonnay	Tawny Port

Chefs on this side of the Atlantic are using tea infusions for subtle flavors in fruit soups and salads, savory dishes, desserts and smoothies. One restaurant in New York City had the first tea sommelier, who would pair teas with each course of your meal. In place of wine, I asked this unique sommelier to select the teas to accompany my dinner. He infused a large quantity of tea leaves for a short specific time in spring water. My dining companions were soon asking to share a cup of my fragrant infusions.

Bubble tea has become the rage, crossing over from Taiwan where it became a hit with teenagers. Large flavored tapioca balls are combined with a powdered mix and brewed tea. This concoction is then drunk through a very large straw in order to crunch down on the tapioca for an interesting tea experience.

Tea Flavored Dishes

Darjeeling/Ginger Tea Syrup for Fresh Fruit

Poached Fish in Keemun Broth

Chai Crème Caramel

Darjeeling/Ginger Tea Syrup for Fresh Fruit

1	tablespoon Darjeeling tea leaves
1	cup boiling water
1	orange, zest only
1	grapefruit, zest only
1	lemon, zest only
1	cup sugar
1	slice of gingerroot, julienned
4	cups fresh fruit, orange and grapefruit sections, melon
	Mixed berries

❋ Infuse the tea leaves with the boiling water for 5 minutes; strain into saucepan. Blanch citrus zests in boiling water 3 times to remove any bitterness.

❋ Add sugar and gingerroot to the tea and bring to the boil. Add the citrus zests and boil until translucent. Cool.

❋ Pour tea infused citrus zests over the fresh fruit. Garnish with fresh mint.

Yields: 8 servings.

Note: Another delicious variation is to use fruit/cinnamon-flavored tea.

Julie Dannenbaum, a cooking teacher at The Gritti Palace in Italy, demonstrated a compote of fruits which was an inspiration for this dish.

Poached Fish in Keemun Broth

2	**teaspoons Keemun tea leaves**
1	**cup boiling water**
1	**shallot, chopped**
4	**salmon fillets, 6 ounces each, skinned, deboned**
1	**cup arugula, destemmed, chopped crosswise**
½	**cup whipping cream**
	Salt and freshly ground white pepper to taste

❀ Infuse tea leaves with boiling water for 5 minutes; strain into sauté pan. Place over medium high heat and add the shallot. Cook for 1 minute. Add the salmon fillets, skin-side down. Cover pan and lower heat to medium. Poach fish for 5 minutes and remove to platter. Reduce tea infusion by half and add the cream; reduce by half once again. Add the arugula and season with salt and pepper. Surround fish with sauce.

Yields: 4 servings.

A three-star restaurant in France created a salmon dish with sorrel that became a classic of nouvelle cuisine. With a surfeit of arugula in my garden, I tried it as a substitute for the sorrel and found it to be quite wonderful.

105

Chai Crème Caramel

8   tablespoons granulated sugar

2   tablespoons water

1   tablespoon Chai spice tea leaves

1   cup boiling water

1   cup whole milk

½   cup granulated sugar

4   large eggs

❀ Place sugar and water in heavy based pan or a copper sugar pot. Bring to boil and let boil until the mixture starts to darken. Immediately pour into 4-cup caramel mold, either metal or a soufflé dish. Cool.

❀ Preheat oven to 350 degrees F. Place a baking pan with water in oven.

❀ Infuse Chai tea leaves with boiling water for 5 minutes; strain into saucepan and add the milk. Bring to a boil. Whisk sugar and eggs together. Pour over the hot milk mixture whisking all the while.

❀ Strain over caramel. Place mold in baking pan and bake 20 to 25 minutes; until a skin like a drum forms on top. Remove from oven and cool.

❀ Refrigerate overnight. Unmold on serving plate and cut pie-shaped wedges to serve. May garnish with fresh strawberries.

Yields: 8 servings.

*Using Chef LeCour's
basic crème caramel,
I spiced it up a bit.*

Holiday Tea Menus

A rare 18th century mahogany cheese cradle, top left, and a Wedgwood tricolor jasper cheese keeper, circa 1860, in green, yellow and white with a silver cheese scoop are the serving pieces with the focus on Stilton and Derby Sage cheeses.

Holiday Tea Menus

Christmas

During the holiday season I showcase my collection of antique British cheese keepers by serving hearty tea savoury dishes with English cheeses as the main ingredient. My collection started during the time we lived in London during the early 1970's and includes jasper ware, majolica, floral Victorian and even a wooden cheese cradle. Victoria magazine featured my collection along with the following recipes in their October 1992 issue.

Holiday Savoury High Tea

English Cheddar Scones with Pub Mustard and Ham

Welsh Rarebit

Tomato Tart with Cheddar

Cheddar and Date Nut Bread

Wensleydale Apple Cake

Stilton Cheesecake with Sliced Pears

English Ale

Hot Rum Punch

Wedgwood olive green cheese stand, 1883, with white bas-relief figures of muses and cherubs, overlooks a Bavarian gold-rimmed plate of savory cheeses.

English Cheddar Scones with Pub Mustard and Ham

1¼	cups self-rising flour
½	teaspoon salt
¼	teaspoon white pepper
½	teaspoon dry mustard
½	cup whole wheat flour
4	tablespoons unsalted butter, plus butter to grease baking sheet
1½	cups grated strong Cheddar cheese
½	cup milk plus 1 tablespoon (for brushing tops of scones)
¼	cup English mustard
6	slices boiled ham

❀ Preheat oven to 425 degrees F. Grease baking sheet. Sift self-rising flour, salt, white pepper and dry mustard into large mixing bowl; stir in whole wheat flour. Cut in butter with a pastry blender until mixture is like coarse meal. Add cheese and toss. Stir in milk and mix just to combine. Use your hand to bring the mixture together to form a ball.

❀ On floured board pat dough to ½-inch thickness. Cut in 2-inch rounds with a sharp biscuit cutter. Place on baking sheet and brush tops with milk. Bake 10 to 12 minutes until golden. Remove from oven and place scones on wire rack to cool. Split scones and spread with English mustard. Sandwich with thinly sliced boiled ham.

Yields: 12 scones.

Note: Recipe may be doubled and scones cut smaller for hors d'oeuvres. Nice to make a walnut butter spread in place of the mustard and serve open-face. Pairs with sherry nicely.

A dear British friend, Grace Falvey, provided the inspiration for this delicious scone by sharing her prize-winning recipe for Cheddar Scones. I adapted her version and used whole-wheat flour for a nutty taste.

Welsh Rarebit

2   cups (8 ounces) Double Gloucester Cheddar cheese

¼   cup ale

2   tablespoons milk

1   teaspoon English mustard

     Freshly ground black pepper

8   slices whole wheat bread, toasted

1   tablespoon unsalted butter, softened

     Pickles and sliced tomatoes for garnish

❁ Place cheese, ale and milk in heavy saucepan or in top of a double boiler. Stir over low heat until mixture is like cream. Add mustard and a dash of freshly grated black pepper.

❁ Butter toast and place on ovenproof serving dish. Pour the melted cheese mixture over toast and place under hot broiler until cheese browns.

❁ Garnish with pickles and sliced tomatoes with ale as the beverage.

Yields: 8 servings.

The cheese of choice for this is Double Gloucester but Cheshire Cheddar works equally as well.

Tomato Tart with Cheddar

Pastry:

1⅔	cups unbleached all-purpose flour
	Pinch of salt
4	ounces unsalted butter, cold
1	large egg
4	tablespoons ice water

Filling:

1	tablespoon English mustard
2	medium-size tomatoes, blanched and peeled
3	large eggs
1	cup heavy cream
¼	teaspoon salt
	Freshly ground white pepper
½	cup grated Sage Derby cheese

❀ Place flour and salt in work bowl of food processor and pulse to blend. Cut butter into 8 equal pieces and add to processor. Process just to mix. Whisk egg and ice water together. With processor running, add egg and water; process until dough comes together. Wrap dough in plastic wrap, flatten into a circle and refrigerate 30 minutes.

❀ Preheat oven to 400 degrees F. Roll pastry out on floured surface to fit a 10-inch round tart pan. Roll pastry slightly larger so sides will be thicker. Prick bottom with a fork.

❀ Paint pastry bottom with mustard. Slice tomatoes and line pastry and pressing tomatoes slightly with a fork.

❀ In bowl, whisk eggs with cream, salt and pepper. Pour over tomatoes and sprinkle with cheese. Bake in oven for 35 to 40 minutes or until filling is set. Remove from oven and let tart rest for 10 minutes. Serve warm.

Yields: 8 servings.

*Daniele Delpeuch,
former personal chef to Mitterand,
taught this recipe in a cooking
class at my school.*

Cheddar and Date Nut Bread

½	cup chopped dried dates
1	cup hot strong tea
2	cups self-rising flour
½	teaspoon salt
1	tablespoon sugar
1	teaspoon baking soda
¼	cup unsalted butter
½	cup Cheshire Cheddar cheese, grated
½	cup chopped walnuts
1	large egg, beaten

❀ In small bowl, soak dates in hot tea for 1 hour. Preheat oven to 325 degrees F. Butter and flour 9 x 5 x 3-inch loaf pan. Line bottom with parchment paper.

❀ In large mixing bowl, sift flour with salt, sugar and baking soda. Use a pastry blender to cut in butter evenly to resemble coarse meal. Add cheese and walnuts, tossing to mix.

❀ Drain tea from dates and save tea. Add dates to flour mixture. Toss to mix.

❀ Whisk egg with tea and add to flour mixture. Stir to combine quickly. Spread batter in loaf pan. Bake 45 minutes or until skewer inserted in center comes out clean.

❀ Cool in pan for 5 minutes. Turn out on wire rack to cool.

Yields: 20 slices.

I make an opal basil jelly that is delicious spread on this bread.

Wensleydale Apple Cake

Cake:

2	**cups all-purpose flour**
¼	**teaspoon salt**
1½	**teaspoons baking powder**
½	**cup granulated sugar**
4	**ounces unsalted butter**
1	**cooking apple, peeled and grated**
1	**large egg**
¼	**cup milk**

Topping:

½	**cup grated Wensleydale cheese**
2	**cooking apples, peeled, cored and sliced**
2	**tablespoons brown sugar**
½	**teaspoon ground cinnamon**
1	**tablespoon unsalted butter**

❁ Preheat oven to 350 degrees F. Butter a deep (2-inch) 8-inch cake springform pan. Line bottom of pan with parchment paper and butter paper.

❁ Sift flour, salt, baking powder and granulated sugar into a large mixing bowl. Use a pastry blender to cut butter into flour mixture. Add grated apple and mix. Set aside.

❁ Whisk egg and milk together in small bowl. Stir into apple mixture to combine. Batter will be stiff. Spread evenly in the pan.

❁ Sprinkle top of cake with the grated cheese. Arrange apple slices on top of cake in a spoke fashion. Combine brown sugar with cinnamon and sprinkle over apples. Dot with the tablespoon of butter.

❁ Bake for 45 to 50 minutes until golden brown. Remove from oven; cool for 5 minutes. Remove sides from pan. Cool cake on wire rack. Remove pan bottom and any parchment paper. Serve cool.

Yields: 10 servings.

This wonderful recipe was shared by my British friend, Lindsey Harman, and it was her mother's tea time treat. Instead of grating all the apples, I sliced one to make the top of the cake more attractive.

A wooden cheese cradle resting on wheels waiting to be rolled down the dining table.

Stilton Cheesecake with Sliced Pears

½	cup walnuts
12	ounces cream cheese, softened
4	ounces unsalted butter, softened
8	ounces Stilton cheese, softened
2	red Bartlett pears, cored and sliced
	Water biscuit crackers

❀ Toast walnuts in 350 degrees F. oven for 8 minutes. Chop finely and set aside. Line a 7-inch springform pan with plastic wrap.

❀ In food processor, combine cream cheese and butter. Pulse to blend. Add crumbled Stilton. Pulse to combine.

❀ Press cheese mixture evenly in springform pan. Cover with plastic wrap and refrigerate until firm.

❀ Remove sides of pan and plastic. Place molded cheese on serving plate. Sprinkle top with walnuts. Surround with crackers and sliced pears.

Yields: 20 servings.

Valentine Tea for Lovers

When we lived in London, a tea dance was a festive affair to announce the engagement of my husband's secretary and I have drawn upon that experience to create a menu for lovers.

Valentine Tea for Lovers

Smoked Salmon Pinwheels

Ham and Asparagus Rollups

Caviar Puffs

Sweetheart Biscuits

Lovers Hazelnut Meringue Heart with Raspberries

Champagne

Sparkling Black Currant Tea Punch (page 175)

Smoked Salmon Pinwheels

6	ounces sliced smoked salmon
8	ounces unsalted butter, softened
1	tablespoon fresh lemon juice
¼	teaspoon ground white pepper
3	ounces cream cheese with chives, softened
1	tablespoon heavy cream
1	pound loaf unsliced bread (brown or white), one day old
1	bunch chives, washed and dried

❀ Place salmon in food processor with half of the butter, lemon juice, white pepper, cream cheese and cream; pulse until smooth.

❀ With serrated bread knife, remove the crust from one long side of the bread. Slice loaf lengthwise into 5 even slices ¼-inch thick. Use part of the remainder of the butter and lightly spread butter on long side of each slice of bread. Remove remaining crusts.

❀ Spread slices evenly with the salmon mixture to within ½-inch of one long side. Roll up tightly from the opposite side and wrap in plastic wrap. Repeat with rest of bread and salmon spread. Refrigerate and filling will firm up.

❀ To serve, remove the plastic wrap and slice into ¼-inch thin pinwheels. Place on serving tray and garnish with freshly chopped chives.

Yields: 60 servings.

These pinwheels lend a luxurious note to your menu and are elegant finger food.

Ham and Asparagus Rollups

1   **pound smoked ham, rind and fat removed, cubed**

1   **pound unsalted butter, softened**

1½   **tablespoons French whole-grain mustard**

1   **tablespoon Worcestershire sauce**

48   **pencil-thin asparagus**

1   **tablespoons salt**

48   **slices of extra-thin white bread**

      Fresh watercress for garnish

❁ In food processor place ham, butter, mustard and Worcestershire; pulse finely.

❁ Trim ends of asparagus. Bring large quantity of water to boil in a large saucepan and add the salt. You can use a tall asparagus steamer if you have it. Lower the asparagus into the water. Return to the boil and boil for 1 minute. Remove asparagus to large bowl of cold water and add ice to keep it bright green and crunchy. Drain and dry well.

❁ Decrust bread with serrated bread knife and spread with ham mixture. Place an asparagus spear on each slice of bread and roll up tightly. Wrap in plastic wrap and refrigerate.

❁ To serve, unwrap rollups. Place rollups in a spoke fashion on a clear crystal cake plate and garnish with fresh watercress.

Yields: 48 servings.

The traditional British potted ham was the inspiration for this piquant sandwich. Garnish with cornichon pickle slices if desired. Men love this combination.

Caviar Puffs

3 ounces unsalted butter, cut into 6 equal pieces

1 cup plus 2 tablespoons water

¼ teaspoon salt

1 cup all-purpose flour, sifted after measuring

4 large eggs

½ cup sour cream

1 tablespoon chopped chives

1 tablespoon fresh lemon juice

4 ounces caviar, golden, red and black

* Preheat oven to 425 degrees F. Dampen 2 baking sheets with cold water. Place butter, water and salt into medium-size pan and bring to a boil over medium heat. The butter should be melted. Remove from the heat.

* Add the flour, all at once, stirring vigorously with a wooden spoon. Return to the heat stirring to dry the mixture. Stir until it leaves the sides of the pan and forms a ball. Remove from the heat and place in a food processor. Turn processor on for 10 seconds to cool the pastry a bit.

* Break eggs, one at a time, into a measuring cup and beat with a fork. Turn food processor on and add egg slowly. Process until egg is absorbed. Repeat with remaining eggs. Mixture should be thick, shiny and smooth.

* Fit a pastry bag with a plain 1-inch round decorating tip and spoon the pastry into the bag. Twist top of pastry bag to close. Pipe 1-inch rounds evenly on baking sheets leaving 1-inch between each for expansion. Dip your thumb in cold water and slightly flatten each tip.

* Place in preheated oven and bake for 12 to 15 minutes, until golden. Do not open the oven door during the initial baking. Remove from oven and use either sharp small knife or a ½-inch decorating tip to make a hole in the top of each puff to allow steam to escape.

❀ Turn oven off and place puffs back in oven with oven door slightly ajar for 2 minutes to dry out the interior of the puffs. Remove puffs from oven and place on a wire rack to cool.

❀ In a bowl mix sour cream with chives and lemon juice. Before serving, fill each puff with a teaspoon of the cream mixture and top with the caviar. Do not fill too far in advance or puffs will become soggy. Serve on a silver platter.

Yields: 36 puffs.

Note: The puff paste dough may be beaten in an electric mixer bowl with the paddle or you may beat the eggs in by hand.

With all the domestic choices of caviar, you can make these a colorful, sparkling presentation. Garnish with lemon roses made from the rind. The choux pastry comes from my classes in Normandy with Chef LeCour, an inspirational teacher.

Sweetheart Biscuits

White Sable Pastry:

8	ounces unsalted butter plus 3 tablespoons, softened
1½	cups granulated sugar
2	large egg yolks
1	tablespoon heavy cream
2⅔	cups all-purpose flour, sifted after measuring

Chocolate Sable Pastry:

8	ounces unsalted butter plus 3 tablespoons, softened
1½	cups granulated sugar
2	large egg yolks
1	tablespoon heavy cream
2	cups all-purpose flour, sifted after measuring
1	scant cup cocoa powder, Dutch processed

I adapted a classic French Pâté Sable dough from a class I had with a chef in the early days of the James Beard Foundation.

❀ For white sable pastry, use electric mixer bowl fitted with flat paddle; cream butter and sugar. Beat in egg yolks and cream. Stir in flour and mix well. For the chocolate sable pastry, sift the flour and cocoa together before adding it to the creamed mixture and mix well.

❀ Shape dough into 2 rolls, each 1-inch in diameter and place together to form one roll. Wrap in plastic and refrigerate until firm but not hard. Dough may be frozen at this point for future use.

❀ Preheat oven to 375 degrees F. Line baking sheets with parchment paper. Slice rolls 3/16-inch thick and cut each with sweetheart cutter. Place hearts on baking sheets and bake for 10 minutes or until the white sable dough is golden. Remove from oven and let stand a bit to firm up.

❀ Remove from baking sheets while still warm to cool on wire racks. Cool and store in airtight tins. Delicious served with chocolate dipped strawberries.

Yields: 60 hearts.

Note: Reform the leftover strips of pastry into a single roll that will be marbled. Chill and cut in 3/16-inch slices to bake.

Lovers' Hazelnut Meringue Heart with Fresh Raspberries

1	tablespoon unsalted butter, softened
1	tablespoon granulated sugar
1	tablespoon all-purpose flour
1	cup shelled hazelnuts
4	egg whites
¾	cup granulated sugar
½	teaspoon white vinegar
1½	cups whipping cream
1	tablespoon confectioners' sugar
½	teaspoon vanilla
1	pint fresh raspberries

I first tasted this delectable confection at a British New Year's Eve party where the hostess was a Cordon Bleu graduate. She traded her recipe for my brownie one and we were both satisfied. The best results are obtained with fresh raspberries.

❧ Grease 2 (8-inch) heart-shaped pans with butter and line bottoms with parchment paper, also buttered. Sprinkle parchment and sides of pans with granulated sugar; then flour and tap out any excess flour.

❧ Preheat oven to 375 degrees F. Place hazelnuts on baking sheet and toast 8 to 10 minutes. Remove from oven and wrap in a kitchen tea towel. Rub nuts with towel to remove the skins. Grind nuts in a food processor with 1 tablespoon granulated sugar to a fine powder. Reduce oven to 350 degrees F.

❧ In an electric mixer, fitted with the whisk, whip the egg whites until stiff. Beat in 2 tablespoons of the granulated sugar and whip 1 minute more. Beat in the vinegar. Combine sugar with nuts. Use three folds to fold into egg whites. Spoon into the cake pans. Bake for 25 to 30 minutes, or until the meringues shrink a bit from the sides of the pans. Remove from oven and allow to cool 5 minutes. Turn out on wire rack to cool completely.

❧ Whip cream in chilled bowl until it starts to thicken. Add the confectioners' sugar and vanilla; whip to a soft shape. Place 1 cake layer on serving plate. Spread a generous layer of cream on top of cake and raspberries on the cream. Top with second cake layer. Crown cake with rosettes of whipped cream using a pastry bag fitted with a ½-inch star tube. Top each rosette with a whole raspberry.

Yields: 10 servings.

Mother's Day Tea

One of my most popular theme teas has been in honor of my mother, who is a wonderful pie and bread baker. On occasion I have offered a Mother/Daughter Tea which rapidly fills up.

Mother's Day Tea

Assorted Tea Sandwiches

Lemon Scones with Strawberry Rose Petal Jam

Orange Curd Tarts

Almond Roll with Fresh Strawberries and Cream

Lemon Thyme Ice Cream

Walnut Biscuit Cake

St. James Blend Tea

Sandwiches

Use breads with a fine crumb that are a day old for easier handling. Spread the filling within the edges of the crust. Use a serrated knife to decrust. To keep sandwiches fresh, cover with damp paper towels and cover with plastic wrap. Refrigerate. If making a day ahead, place cut sandwiches in plastic containers and seal.

Curried Egg Sandwiches

12	**slices extra-thin sandwich white bread**
4	**ounces unsalted butter, softened**
2	**tablespoons chopped chives**
3-4	**tablespoons heavy cream**
¼	**teaspoon curry powder**
4	**hard-cooked eggs, shelled, chopped finely**
	Salt and pepper

Spread sandwich slices with softened butter. Sprinkle 1 slice with chives. Heat 1 tablespoon cream with curry powder and combine with chopped eggs and enough cream to make a smooth spread. Season with salt and pepper. Spread 1 slice of bread with egg filling and place on top of other slice. Decrust. Slice into fingers.

Yields: 24 fingers.

For an elegant presentation, arrange sandwiches on frosted glass round plates with edible flowers or herbs as dividers of the various types. This is a particularly creamy egg filling.

Stilton Cheese and Watercress Squares

12	slices extra-thin white bread
4	ounces unsalted butter, softened
8	ounces Stilton cheese, softened
	Bunch of watercress, washed and dried

 Spread bread with butter. Cover half the slices with the Stilton and top with watercress sprigs. Press bread slices together and decrust. Cut into squares.

Yields: 24 squares.

> *Seek out a farmhouse Stilton as it will be really creamy.*

Turkey and Cranberry Triangles

4	ounces unsalted butter, softened
12	slices extra-thin white bread
1	tablespoon cranberry jelly
8	ounces sliced turkey

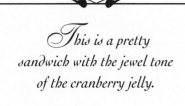 Mix softened butter and cranberry jelly together. Spread on bread and top with the turkey slices on half the bread. Press bread slices together and decrust. Cut into triangles.

Yields: 24 triangles.

> *This is a pretty sandwich with the jewel tone of the cranberry jelly.*

Smoked Trout Sandwiches

12	slices extra-thin whole-wheat sandwich bread
4	ounces unsalted butter, softened
6	ounces smoked trout, skinned, bone removed
4	tablespoons mayonnaise
1	tablespoon fresh lemon juice
¼	cup watercress leaves

❀ Spread bread with butter. Combine smoked trout, mayonnaise and lemon juice to taste in blender. Spread bread with smoked fish filling. Sprinkle with watercress leaves. Top with second slice of bread. Decrust and cut into triangles.

Yields: 24 triangles.

The original recipe used smoked haddock but smoked trout is a favorite of my husband's so I changed it up to suit him.

Lemon Scones with Rose Petal Jam

2   **cups unbleached all-purpose flour**

1   **cup cake flour**

½   **cup granulated sugar plus 2 tablespoons**

1   **tablespoon plus 1 teaspoon baking powder**

½   **teaspoon salt**

1   **large egg, beaten**

1   **cup heavy cream plus 1 tablespoon**

1   **teaspoon grated lemon zest**

    Devon cream

Preheat oven to 450 degrees F. Line baking sheet with parchment paper. Combine flours, ½ cup sugar, baking powder and salt in mixing bowl. Stir in egg, cream and lemon zest into dry ingredients to just moisten. Turn dough out onto lightly floured work surface and divide in half. Shape each half into a 6-inch disk. With sharp knife, cut each disk into 6 wedges. Place wedges ½-inch apart on baking sheet. Brush tops with cream and sprinkle with granulated sugar. Bake until golden, 12 to 15 minutes. Remove from oven and cool.

Yields: 12 scones.

Note: Serve with Rose Petal Jam and Devon cream.

A light and creamy scone due to the cream

Rose Petal Jam

2   pounds strawberries, washed and hulled

½   cup fresh rose petals, pesticide free, washed

2   tablespoons fresh lemon juice

2   pounds granulated sugar

❀ Place berries in heavy non-reactive deep preserving pan. Mash lightly and bring to boil. Cut off the hearts of the rose petals as they are bitter. When the berries are translucent, add rose petals, lemon juice and sugar. Boil rapidly until jam reaches the setting stage which is 214 degrees F. (on jelly thermometer).

❀ Ladle into sterilized jars. Top off with melted paraffin and seal with lids.

Yields: 4 half-pints.

In my garden, I grow old English roses that are very fragrant and pesticide free.

Swiss Roll with Almond Filling and Fresh Strawberries

Swiss Roll:

1	**tablespoon shortening**
1	**tablespoon all-purpose flour**
1	**cup sifted cake flour**
¾	**teaspoon baking powder**
¼	**teaspoon salt**
4	**large eggs**
1	**cup granulated sugar**
1	**teaspoon vanilla**
⅓	**cup water**

Almond Filling:

¼	**cup slivered almonds, toasted at 350 degrees F., 8 to 10 minutes**
1	**cup whipping cream, chilled and whipped, 1 tablespoon sugar to taste**
1	**pound fresh strawberries, washed and hulled**

I adapted this cake from my mentor, Flo Braker, who taught it in a cooking class. Her technique for splitting the cake works wonderfully.

❀ Preheat oven to 400 degrees F. Line a 10 x 15 x 1-inch baking sheet with foil. Lightly grease foil with shortening and sprinkle with flour. Shake to cover evenly.

❀ Sift flour, baking powder and salt together onto wax paper. Break eggs into bowl of mixer fitted with wire whisk. Whisk eggs to lighten them. With mixer running, add the sugar and whip until light in color.

❀ Using a large rubber spatula, carefully fold in the flour. Add the vanilla and water. Pour batter onto the prepared pan and spread it evenly. Bake for 10 to 12 minutes, or until golden. Remove cake from oven to a wire rack to cool.

❀ Remove cake with its foil from the baking pan. Trim any crisp edges with serrated knife. Split cake horizontally into two very thin layers using a serrated knife around the edges to start and finish with a ham slicing knife to cut all the way through. Carefully flip 1 layer upward and overlap the two layers ¼-inch.

❀ For the filling, fold the toasted almonds into the whipped cream. Spread Swiss roll with almond cream. Slice strawberries and place on cream. Roll up the confection and chill before serving. Sprinkle with confectioners' sugar and garnish with whole strawberries. Use serrated knife to serve.

Yields: 12 slices.

Lemon Thyme Ice Cream

2 cups whole milk

1 cup whipping cream

¾ cup granulated sugar

3 egg yolks

1 tablespoon fresh lemon thyme leaves, crushed

Bring milk and cream to boil in saucepan; add sugar, stirring well and bring back to boil. Whisk egg yolks in mixing bowl, add milk mixture slowly to temper egg yolks. Add thyme leaves and let cool. Strain into bowl and chill. Freeze in ice-cream machine for 25 to 30 minutes. Let ripen in freezer for 2 hours and serve with the Swiss Roll.

Yields: 1 quart.

A famous French chef in Dallas made a variety of infused ice creams and went on to found a company called, Out of a Flower. I developed this recipe after tasting his at a dinner.

Filo Pastry Tarts with Orange Curd

Orange Curd:

4	tablespoons unsalted butter
½	cup confectioners' sugar
2	large eggs
⅓	cup freshly squeezed orange juice
½	cup orange marmalade
½	cup cream, whipped

❀ Cook butter and confectioners' sugar together over low heat in heavy pan. Whisk eggs and slowly drizzle them into pan, whisking constantly. Cook until thick; stirring all the while. Whisk in orange juice. Cool.

❀ Spread a teaspoon of orange marmalade in bottom of tarts. Fill with orange curd and top with whipped cream.

Yields: 30 tarts.

Bake the filo tart recipe from the Fairy Tea Menu and fill with the orange curd.

Chocolate Walnut Biscuit Cake

4	tablespoons unsalted butter
3	tablespoons corn syrup (golden treacle in Great Britain)
7	ounces semi-sweet or bittersweet chocolate
7	ounces digestive biscuits (Carr)
2	tablespoons raisins
2	tablespoons toasted walnuts, finely chopped

❀ Line a 7-inch square pan with foil and grease the foil. Melt butter with syrup. Separately melt the chocolate. Crush biscuits in food processor. Place in a mixing bowl and add the butter, syrup and melted chocolate. Fold in the raisins. Turn mixture into pan and smooth top. Sprinkle with the walnuts. Cover with plastic wrap and refrigerate to firm up.

Yields: 12 squares.

My first fundraising attempt was a tasting of British and American foods in England to benefit the deaf for a weekend at the seashore. We raised enough money for them to spend two weeks at the shore. This recipe was contributed by a British lady who was deaf but not handicapped when it came to cooking.

"...her expression grew serious, worried, petulant because she was afraid of missing the flower show, or merely of not being in time for tea, with muffins and toast, at the Rue Royale tearooms, where she believed that regular attendance was indispensable in order to set the seal upon a woman's certificate of elegance..."

Swann in Love,
Marcel Proust

Bastille Day

The French equivalent of our Fourth of July can be the occasion for a festive, hearty tea. Put up a French flag and invite some French friends to celebrate.

Bastille Day Tea

Pistachio and Artichoke Pâté

Salmon Pâté

Cornichons and Radishes

Daniel's Walnut Slices

Financiers

Normandy Chocolate Gâteau

French Cheeses

French Breads

Apple Infusion Tea

Rosé Champagne

An outfitted leather picnic travel case replete with sardine and pâté molds, serving dishes, flatware and reed wrapped condiment pieces serves as the carrier for the picnic fare atop the bamboo tea table. A Mason's Ironstone Cheese Keeper, 1880, with peonies is the highlight for the French cheeses.

Pistachio and Artichoke Pâté

¼   **cup shelled pistachios**

1   **14-ounce can artichoke hearts,
drained, rinsed**

4   **ounces unsalted butter, softened**

1   **tablespoon fresh lemon juice**

In work bowl of food processor, chop the nuts coarsely. Add the artichoke hearts, butter and lemon juice; pulse to combine. Spread on French bread.

Yields: 2 cups.

*This is a colorful pâté
as well as a tasty one.*

Smoked Salmon Pâté

10   ounces smoked salmon

4   tablespoons unsalted butter

4   ounces cream cheese

2   tablespoons sour cream

1   tablespoon fresh lemon juice

½   teaspoon ground mace

     **Salt and freshly ground white
       pepper**

¼   cup clarified butter

❖ Puree fish in blender or food processor. Mix in remaining ingredients except the clarified butter. Spoon into crockery mold and pour over a thin film of clarified butter. Cover with plastic wrap and refrigerate.

❖ Remove from refrigerator 1 hour before serving. Serve with French bread. May be kept sealed two weeks in refrigerator and frozen up to two months.

Yields: 1½ cups.

*A nice pâté to have on hand
as it keeps and improves with age.*

Daniel's Walnut Slices

Base:

¾	cup all-purpose flour
1	teaspoon baking powder
½	cup granulated sugar
2	cups ground walnuts
4	tablespoons unsalted butter
4	large eggs, separated
	Pinch of salt

Topping:

8	ounces semi-sweet chocolate
4	tablespoons unsalted butter

❋ Preheat oven to 350 degrees F. Butter a 10 x 15 x 1-inch jelly-roll pan. In food processor fitted with steel blade, process flour, baking powder, sugar and ground walnuts until mixed. Incorporate butter and egg yolks.

❋ Add salt to egg whites and beat until stiff. Gently fold egg whites into flour mixture with spatula. Spread batter out to ¼-inch thickness in pan. Bake for 20 to 25 minutes.

❋ Melt chocolate and butter in heavy pan over low heat on stove. Spread over top of walnut slices with spatula. Decorate with walnut halves if desired. Cut into 12 equal squares.

Yields: 12 servings.

The first time Daniel Delpeuch came to teach for me, she taught this dessert from the southwest of France where walnuts abound.

Fianciers

10 tablespoons unsalted butter

½ cup ground almonds or almond paste

1 cup confectioners' sugar, sifted

½ cup all-purpose flour

2 large egg whites

❀ Preheat oven to 425 degrees F. Melt butter and brown slightly. In mixing bowl, combine almonds, sugar and flour. Stir in the butter and then the egg whites. Refrigerate for 1 hour to firm up the batter.

❀ Butter oval frangipane molds. Half fill each mold; place on baking sheet. Bake for 5 minutes; turn oven down to 400 degrees F. Bake for 5 to 8 minutes, until golden. Remove from oven and turn out onto parchment paper.

Yields: 24 financiers.

A delightful almond tart that can be served with fresh fruit. Try these at Angelina, opened in 1903, after shopping the rue de Rivoli in Paris.

Normandy Chocolate Gâteau

7	ounces unsalted butter
8	ounces semi-sweet chocolate, grated
4	large eggs, separated
¾	cup granulated sugar
½	cup all-purpose flour, sifted
	Pinch of salt
	Confectioners' sugar for sprinkling cake

❀ Preheat oven to 350 degrees F. Butter and flour 9-inch cake pan. Line bottom with parchment paper.

❀ In double boiler, melt butter and chocolate together. In mixing bowl, whisk egg yolks and sugar together to lighten; add flour. Add a bit of the chocolate mixture to temper the egg yolks; then add the rest of the melted chocolate and butter; stirring well.

❀ Whisk egg whites with pinch of salt until stiff. Fold into the batter. Pour into prepared pan and bake for 20 minutes. Remove from oven and cool for 10 minutes. Turn out on wire rack to cool. Remove parchment paper. Sift confectioners' sugar over the top.

Yields: 10 servings.

This recipe comes from Chef LeCour who taught Normandy cuisine in Dieppe. He managed to get 84 tastes out of this recipe.

Special Occasion Teas

A visit by the Queen calls for the brilliance of a Waterford cut glass cheese keeper with a Georgian cheese scoop to serve the Stilton. Limoges gold-banded teacups await the Coronation tea. The deep rose carries through in the etched glass window and is echoed in the punch.

Special Occasion Teas

"I did send for a cup of tea of which I had never drank before."

Pepys's Diary, 1660

When I received the call to advise on tea for the Queen of England on her first trip to Texas, I immediately created a menu showcasing Texas products. I then contacted an English friend who is in and out of Buckingham Palace on a regular basis for I knew she would be able to enlighten me as to the likes and dislikes of Her Majesty. She thought my menu was absolutely perfect. What the Queen would have thought I will never know for a simple reception was chosen instead. However, two Texas food editors wrote stories about my menu.

Queen's Tea Southwest Style

Smoked Texas Turkey Triangles with Marigold Mint Butter

Tomato Rounds with Opal Basil Butter
and Texas Goat Cheese

Begonia Sandwiches

Cured Salmon in Filo Cups with Cucumber Sesame Salsa

Cinnamon Basil Scones with Texas Blackberry Jam

Texas Pecan Shortbread

Lemon Cheese Tarts with Texas Blueberries

Queen of Sheba Chocolate Cake

Southwest Spiced Tea Punch (page 177)

Coronation Tea

Smoked Texas Turkey Triangles
with Marigold Mint Butter

8   **ounces smoked turkey breast**

½   **cup mayonnaise**

     Freshly ground white pepper

4   **ounces unsalted butter, softened**

1   **tablespoon chopped marigold mint, blossoms for garnish**

12   **slices extra-thin whole wheat sandwich bread**

❧ Place turkey, cut into chunks, into a blender or food processor and add the mayonnaise. Blend to fine consistency and season with the white pepper.

❧ In bowl cream the butter and add the mint. Spread the mint butter on one side of the bread slices. Spread half the bread slices with the turkey filling. Sandwich together and decrust the bread. Cut into triangles. Garnish with marigold mint blossoms.

Yields: 24 triangles.

Be sure to use a premium brand of smoked turkey breast so this will not be oversalted.

Tomato Rounds with
Opal Basil Butter and Texas Goat Cheese

2	large tomatoes, peeled, deseeded and finely diced
4	ounces unsalted butter, softened
1	tablespoon finely chopped opal basil
10	slices extra-thin white sandwich bread
4	ounces goat cheese, chilled
	Basil leaves for garnish

Drain tomatoes in sieve. Combine butter with opal basil and spread bread slices on one side. Using a 1½-inch fluted cutter, cut out 4 rounds per slice of bread. Top each round with tomatoes.

Slice goat cheese into ¼-inch slices. Use a cake decorating tube to cut ½-inch rounds from the goat cheese slices. Place on top of tomatoes and garnish with small opal basil leaf.

Yields: 40 rounds.

Texas is fortunate to have Paula Lambert of The Mozzarella Company producing award winning goat cheese. Because of her fine product, I created this taste treat for a tea class.

Begonia Sandwiches

6   **extra-thin slices white bread**

2   **ounces unsalted butter, softened**

48   **edible begonia blossoms**

 Spread bread slices on one side with butter and decrust. Top with the begonia blossoms and slice in 4 triangles. Arrange on sandwich tray and garnish with more begonias.

Yields: 24 triangles.

Edible flowers such as roses, marigolds, nasturtiums and begonias are often used in English tea sandwiches during the summer. The blossoms must be non-toxic and pesticide-free for safety's sake.

Cured Salmon in Filo Cups with Cucumber Sesame Salsa

¼	cup rock salt
½	cup granulated sugar
½	teaspoon ground white peppercorns
12	ounces fresh salmon fillet without skin
6	filo pastry sheets
4	ounces unsalted sweet butter, melted
½	cup burpless cucumber, peeled, deseeded and diced finely
½	red jalapeño pepper, deseeded and minced
1	teaspoon minced fresh ginger
1	teaspoon sugar
½	teaspoon sesame oil
4	ounces sour cream

✿ Combine rock salt with sugar and ground peppercorns. Place salmon on plastic wrap and rub salt, sugar and pepper mixture over salmon. Wrap with plastic wrap and refrigerate 6 hours to cure. Weight with brick wrapped in foil. After salmon has cured, wash well and dry.

✿ Unfold pastry sheets and place one sheet on pastry surface. Paint pastry sheet with melted butter. Top with remaining pastry sheets, painting each sheet with butter. Cut out 1⅞-inch fluted rounds and line mini-muffin pans with pastry buttered side down. Prick bottoms with fork; freeze 10 minutes.

✿ Preheat oven to 375 degrees F. Bake pastry rounds on baking trays for 5 minutes. Remove from oven and press out bubbles with flat side of teaspoon. Return to oven for 4 minutes to bake until golden. Turn out to cool on wire rack. Combine diced cucumber, jalapeño pepper, ginger, sugar and sesame oil for salsa. Place rounded teaspoon of sour cream in each pastry round, top with cucumber salsa and thinly sliced salmon formed into rosettes.

Yields: 40 appetizers.

My following recipe took a prize in a national competition for professional chefs. The grand prizewinner turned out to be award-winning Chef Victor Gielisse, a friend, and we taught our prize dishes in a cooking class at my school.

Cinnamon Basil Scones

3	cups unbleached all-purpose flour
1½	tablespoons baking powder
1	teaspoon baking soda
1	teaspoon salt
2	tablespoons granulated sugar
½	teaspoon ground cinnamon
1	tablespoon chopped fresh basil or 1 teaspoon dried
4	ounces unsalted butter
¾	cup buttermilk
2	tablespoons milk
1	cup heavy cream, whipped
1	jar blackberry jam

❀ Preheat oven to 425 degrees F. Grease baking sheet with 1 tablespoon butter.

❀ Sift the dry ingredients into a large mixing bowl. Toss in the chopped basil. Cut in the butter with a pastry blender or your finger-tips until mixture resembles large pea-sized pebbles.

❀ Make a well in center and add the butter-milk. Use a large wooden spoon to mix the dough. Turn out on a lightly floured work surface and knead lightly. Roll dough to ½-inch thickness. Cut into 2-inch squares. Place on baking sheet close together.

❀ Brush tops with milk and bake for 10 to 12 minutes or until golden. Remove from oven and serve with whipped cream and jam.

Yields: 2 dozen scones.

This scone is a wonderful base for a berry shortcake dessert.

Texas Pecan Shortbread

8	ounces unsalted butter, softened
½	cup superfine sugar
2¼	cups all-purpose flour
¼	cup pecans, broken pieces

Preheat oven to 325 degrees F. In food processor place butter, sugar, flour and pecans. Process to bring together. Turn out on plastic wrap and chill 10 minutes. Place on baking sheet lined with parchment paper.

Draw 3 (7-inch) circles on parchment lined baking sheet and press dough in even rounds forming a fluted edge. Prick with fork and score each round into 8 petticoat fingers. Chill 15 minutes.

Bake 10 to 12 minutes or just until edges are golden. Remove from oven and let stand about 2 minutes. Slice through scored rounds. Place shortbread on cooling racks. Store in airtight containers.

Yields: 24 fingers.

My ancestors settled in Ellinger, Texas, where marvelous, flavorful native pecans grow on the Colorado River bottom land.

Lemon Cheese Tarts with Texas Blueberries

Pastry:

2	cups unbleached flour
½	teaspoon baking powder
1	tablespoon sugar
	Pinch salt
1	tablespoon chopped mint
4	ounces unsalted butter
6	tablespoons ice water
1	teaspoon lemon juice

✤ Preheat oven to 375 degrees F. Place flour, baking powder, sugar, salt and mint in food processor bowl. Combine water and lemon juice in measuring cup. Process butter with flour and add water and lemon juice. Refrigerate 30 minutes.

✤ Roll out thinly and cut into 1¾-inch fluted rounds. Fit into tart tins or muffin pans. Prick with fork. Bake with a blind of beans or pie weights for 10 to 12 minutes, until golden. Remove to wire rack to cool.

Lemon Cheese Filling:

8	ounces cream cheese, softened
½	cup sour cream
¼	cup sugar
1½	teaspoons lemon zest
1	box of blueberries, washed and dried

✤ In mixing bowl combine cream cheese with sour cream, sugar and lemon zest. Fill tarts with cream mixture. Top each with one blueberry.

Yields: 24 tarts.

In East Texas, many varieties of blueberries are grown.

Queen of Sheba Chocolate Cake

Cake:

1	**tablespoon unsalted butter**
4	**ounces extra bittersweet chocolate, chopped**
4	**ounces unsalted butter, softened**
3	**egg yolks**
4	**egg whites**
⅔	**cup granulated sugar, divided**
½	**teaspoon vanilla**
1	**cup ground blanched almonds**
⅓	**cup all-purpose flour**
10	**whole toasted blanched almonds**

Chocolate Glaze:

4	**ounces extra bittersweet chocolate, chopped**
1	**teaspoon peanut oil**

This chocolate delight was a smashing success at the tea I hosted at the James Beard Foundation. Purchase a fine chocolate such as Lindt, Callebaut or Tobler. I favor the Valrhona extra bittersweet for the depth of roasted flavor. Heart-shaped pans may be used for a Valentine's treat and the cake garnished with fresh raspberries.

❀ Preheat oven to 350 degrees F. Grease a 9-inch round springform cake pan with unsalted butter and line bottom with parchment paper, also greased.

❀ Melt chocolate in top of double boiler over simmering water, stirring until smooth. Remove from heat and let cool for 5 minutes.

❀ In a mixing bowl, cream the butter and beat in the cool, soft chocolate. Add egg yolks, one at a time, beating well after each addition. Gradually beat in half of the sugar. Add the vanilla and stir in the ground almonds and flour.

❀ With an electric hand mixer, whip the egg whites until soft peaks form and add the remaining sugar, beating to stiff peaks. Stir one-fourth of the egg whites into the chocolate mixture and lightly fold the remaining whites in with a rubber spatula.

❀ Pour batter into prepared pan and bake 25 to 30 minutes. Do not over bake as the center of the cake should be slightly soft. Cool 5 minutes and turn out onto wire cooling rack. Remove parchment paper and let cool completely. Place on cardboard round or directly on serving plate.

❀ Melt chocolate with peanut oil for glaze and pour over cake. Spread with icing spatula just on the top. Place toasted almonds around the outer top perimeter of the cake.

Yields: 10 slices.

Bridal Shower Tea

Plan a special setting for the bridal party to relax and enjoy your ambiance of fine tea fare. You might consider having each guest bring a teacup for the bride and you can fête her with a teapot. Give a short talk on the etiquette of tea. If you can serve outdoors, your guests could be asked to wear large hats for the sun. I gave such a tea for my friend's daughter and used soft lavender as the color theme. Serving buffet from my dining table enabled me to enjoy the affair as well.

Bridal Shower Tea

Cucumber Hearts

Deviled Salmon Triangles

Herbed Cheese Coeur à la Crème

Fruit Tarts

Roland's Lovers Chocolate Cake

Vintage Darjeeling

Rose Petal Champagne Punch
with Strawberries (page 176)

Cucumber Hearts

4   **ounces unsalted butter, softened**

1   **teaspoon fresh dill, chopped**

10   **slices extra-thin white sandwich bread**

1   **burpless cucumber, scored with a fork**

    Fresh dill for garnish

 Combine butter and chopped dill. Spread one side of bread slices with butter and dill mixture. Cut with 1½-inch heart-shaped cutter. Thinly slice cucumber and arrange on heart bases. Garnish with fresh dill sprigs.

Yields: 40 heart-shaped sandwiches.

This is an eye appealing way of presenting the cucumber sandwich.

Deviled Salmon Pinwheels

10   **slices extra-thin brown sandwich bread**

4   **ounces unsalted butter, softened**

1   **cup cooked salmon**

1   **tablespoon minced chives**

1   **teaspoon Worcestershire sauce**

4   **drops Tabasco hot sauce**

¼   **cup mayonnaise**

1   **tablespoon lemon juice**

    Salt and freshly ground white pepper

 Spread one side of bread with the softened butter. Mix the salmon with the remaining ingredients in food processor. Spread one side of buttered bread and decrust. Roll up tightly and wrap in plastic wrap. Pack closely together in a plastic container, cover and chill.

To serve: Unwrap and slice into 5 pinwheels. You can do 6 if you use an electric knife.

Yields: 48 to 60 pinwheels.

A bit of extra work but worth it for these dainty morsels.

Herbed Cheese Coeur à la Crème

8	ounces cottage cheese, drained
8	ounces cream cheese, softened
8	ounces plain yogurt
1	tablespoon chopped fresh chives
1	tablespoon chopped fresh parsley
1	tablespoon chopped fresh mint
	Fresh chives, mint and parsley for garnish
	Water biscuit crackers

❀ Combine cottage cheese and cream cheese in food processor and process until smooth. Add yogurt, chives, parsley and mint; process just until blended. Line a 7-inch coeur à la crème mold or colander with a double layer of damp cheesecloth. Pour mixture into the mold and fold cheesecloth over the top. Place mold on tray to drain and refrigerate overnight.

❀ To serve: remove cheesecloth and unmold onto serving dish. Surround with the fresh herbs and place chive sprigs in center. Serve with plain biscuit water crackers.

Yields: 1½ cups.

I created this for an hors d'oeuvres Christmas class and adapted it for my bridal shower.

Fruit Tarts

1⅔ cups unbleached all-purpose flour

½ teaspoon baking powder

2 tablespoons sugar

Pinch salt

4 ounces unsalted butter, frozen

1 large egg

4 tablespoons ice water

1 teaspoon lemon juice

½ cup sieved apricot preserves

1 tablespoon water

Fresh strawberries, seedless grapes, bananas, kiwi, raspberries, blueberries

❀ Place flour, baking powder, sugar and salt in work bowl of food processor fitted with steel blade. Pulse quickly to blend. Add butter, cut into 8 equal pieces and pulse with quick on/off 3 to 4 times.

❀ Whisk egg with ice water and lemon juice in a measuring cup with a pouring spout. With food processor running, pour the liquids in the spout and run just to blend. Remove dough from food processor and wrap in plastic wrap. You can use this immediately but I prefer to chill it for 30 minutes for easier handling. The lemon juice tenderizes the pastry.

❀ Preheat oven to 400 degrees F. Roll pastry out on lightly floured marble or wooden surface to ⅛-inch thinness. Use a fluted round pastry cutter that will cut rounds to fit in mini-size tart tins that measure 1½ inches across. Place in tart tins and bake blind with parchment paper weighted with pie weights or beans. Bake 8 to 10 minutes, until golden. Remove from oven and unmold onto wire rack to cool.

❀ Heat sieved apricot preserves with water. Wash fruit and drain on paper towels.

❀ To serve: Brush pastry tarts with apricot glaze and fill with sliced strawberries, seedless grapes, bananas, kiwi or whole raspberries and blueberries. Brush fruit with apricot glaze.

Yields: 4 dozen tarts.

Jean Marie Maudet, a French pastry chef from the Loire, taught this pastry in a class for me when he was living in Dallas. We lost him to a three-star restaurant in London.

Roland's Lovers Chocolate Cake

14   ounces extra-bittersweet baking
       chocolate

14   tablespoons unsalted butter

1½   cups granulated sugar, divided

10   large eggs, separated

2   oranges, zested

       Juice of 1 orange

¼   cup Grand Marnier liquor

       Confectioners' sugar

       Fresh berries for garnish

❁ Preheat oven to 450 degrees F. Butter and flour a 14-inch cake mold or 2 (10-inch) cake pans and line with parchment paper. Break chocolate into equal pieces and melt with the butter in a double boiler. Stir in 1 cup of the sugar and whisk to dissolve. Beat the egg yolks with the orange juice and zest. Beat some of the hot chocolate mixture into the yolks to temper them. Add to the chocolate mixture and stir until thickened. Stir in the Grand Marnier.

❁ Beat the egg whites at a low speed and increase to high, beating to soft peaks. Add the remaining sugar slowly and beat until stiff. Whisk a large dollop of whites into the chocolate mixture to lighten it. Fold the chocolate into the egg whites lightly. Pour into the prepared pans.

❁ Bake 5 minutes at high heat and lower the heat to 250 degrees F. For the large pan, 45 minutes will be the baking time. Check the small pans at 20 minutes. Remove from the oven and cool. Chill overnight.

❁ To serve: unmold cake onto serving plate and remove parchment paper. Sprinkle with sifted confectioners' sugar and garnish with fresh berries. You can also frost with chocolate ganache and chocolate curls for a knockout presentation. Roland now serves it with a mint crème anglaise.

Note: I often bake the two smaller layers and freeze one for later. I have carried this cake from Texas to New York and California and never had it break.

Roland Passot of La Folie in San Francisco and I baked eleven of these flourless wonders for my best friend's 50th birthday. We made them in large round and square shapes. This has become my family's favorite birthday cake.

Yields: 24 servings.

Fairy Tea

When my first granddaughter, Samantha June, came to visit from California, I hosted a tea to introduce her to my friends. I made her a violet print dress and bonnet to match my violet print tea frock and I lined the bassinet with a violet print. She was just three months old. All my tea accouterments were in violet patterns with miniature Cinderella dolls pirouetting on the sides of tea butlers. We played pass the baby once she awakened.

Fairy Tea

Fairy Tea Sandwiches

Hazelnut Shortbread

St. Regis Cranberry Mini-Scones with
Raspberry Jam and Whipped Cream

Orange Madeleines

Milk Chocolate Circus Animals

Fairy Angel Food Delight

Lime Curd Tarts

Violet Tea

Champagne with Stemmed Strawberries

Tea in miniature as a Staffordshire figure sips her tea balanced on the cross rail of an antique Victorian bed overlooking the smallest of Austrian cheese keepers and miniature tea accessories. Royal purple butterflies garnish the fairies' tea fare.

Fairy Tea Sandwiches

Cake:

1	tablespoon unsalted butter
2	cups all-purpose flour
2	teaspoons baking powder
¼	teaspoon salt
3	large eggs
8	ounces unsalted butter, melted
1½	cups granulated sugar
1	teaspoon vanilla extract
⅔	cup milk

Filling:

4	ounces hazelnut spread
2	ounces cream cheese, softened
¼	cup fresh raspberries

❀ Preheat oven to 350 degrees F. Grease a 9 x 5 x 3-inch loaf pan with unsalted butter and line bottom with parchment paper. Sift flour, baking powder and salt onto waxed paper and set aside.

❀ In electric mixer, whisk eggs until fluffy and light; add sugar whisking as you go. Slowly add butter and mix. Add vanilla. With mixer running at low speed, add a third of the dry ingredients; add half the milk. Add a third of the dry ingredients and mix. Add remaining milk and dry ingredients, mixing. Pour batter into pan and bake until cake springs back from sides of pan when touched, 35 to 40 minutes. Remove from oven and cool in pan for 10 minutes. Take cake from pan and cool on wire rack thoroughly.

❀ With electric knife, slice cake into ¼-inch slices. Spread hazelnut spread on one slice and place cake slice on top.

❀ Blend cream cheese and raspberries in food processor. Spread on another slice of cake and sandwich to the first two slices. Decrust. Cut each sandwich into ½-inch fingers. Place on sides so stripes of hazelnut and raspberry filling show.

Yields: 4 dozen.

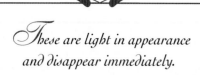

These are light in appearance and disappear immediately.

Hazelnut Shortbread

⅓   **cup hazelnuts, shelled**

1⅔   **cups all-purpose flour**

8   **ounces unsalted butter, softened, plus 1 tablespoon to grease pan**

½   **cup granulated sugar**

¼   **cup confectioners' sugar**

❀ Preheat oven to 350 degrees F. Roast hazelnuts on baking sheet for 8 to 10 minutes. Place nuts on tea towel and rub off skins. In food processor, grind nuts really fine with ⅓ cup of the flour. Add remaining flour and process together.

❀ In large mixing bowl, cream butter and add the sugar. Combine with flour and nut mixture. Wrap shortbread in plastic wrap and chill 30 minutes.

❀ Line 2 cookie sheets with parchment paper. Take a heaping teaspoon of mixture, shape into a ball and place on baking sheet 2 inches apart. Flatten slightly with the thumb and bake 20 minutes. Remove from oven and transfer to a wire rack to cool. Sprinkle with confectioners' sugar.

Yields: 40 shortbread.

A British cookery writer, Suzy Benghiat, made these for me many years ago and shared her recipe. Middle Eastern food is her specialty but these are very special to me.

St. Regis Mini-Cranberry Scones

4	ounces unsalted butter plus 1 tablespoon for greasing pan
1⅓	cups sour cream
3	tablespoons granulated sugar
1⅓	cups plus 2 tablespoons cake flour
1⅓	cups plus 2 tablespoons all-purpose flour
5	teaspoons baking powder
1	teaspoon salt
	Zest of 1 orange
	Zest of 1 lemon
¼	cup dried cranberries
1	tablespoon heavy cream
1	tablespoon granulated sugar
	Raspberry jam
1	cup cream whipped

❀ Preheat oven to 325 degrees F. Butter baking sheet. Cream butter with sour cream and sugar. Sift dry ingredients together. Add orange and lemon zests along with the dried cranberries and toss with flour. Add to the butter, sour cream and sugar mixture and mix.

❀ On floured surface, pat out dough to a round 1½-inch thickness. Use a sharp knife to cut round into 8 triangles. Cut each triangle on the diagonal. Place on baking sheet; brush with cream and sprinkle with sugar. Bake for 25 to 30 minutes. Remove from oven and cool.

❀ To serve, split the scones in half horizontally and cover with raspberry jam and a dollop of whipped cream.

Yields: 16 triangular scones.

My daughter, Emily, once worked for The St. Regis Hotel in New York City where their afternoon tea was my very favorite. I implored Emily to get their scone recipe as two pastry chefs did nothing but make very tall scones and jams for their afternoon tea service. She was able to have them write it down but their recipe made 80 scones. I have reduced it with happy results.

Tea 101 for Fairies Lily and Samantha.

Orange Madeleines

2	tablespoons unsalted butter, melted
2	tablespoons flour
4	large eggs
1¼	cups granulated sugar
1	cup all-purpose flour
	Grated rind of 1 orange
¼	cup unsalted butter, melted until brown
	Confectioners' sugar for sprinkling

✤ Preheat oven to 400 degrees F. Butter small madeleine molds with the melted butter and dust with flour. Invert to tap out any excess flour. Chill.

✤ In mixing bowl, whisk eggs to thicken and gradually add sugar, whisking until pale yellow in color. Mixture will make a ribbon on the surface. Fold in the flour and orange rind. Add the brown butter last. Fill molds ⅔ full. Bake for 8 minutes or until golden. Remove from oven and unmold by knocking mold on the surface counter. Once cool; dust with confectioners' sugar.

Yields: 10 dozen miniature madeleines or 4 dozen regular size.

The cookie of choice for Marcel Proust with his afternoon cuppa.

Milk Chocolate Circus Animals

14   **ounces compound coating,
melting chocolate**

**Circus animal candy molds, clean
and dry**

*You can find the plastic
molds and chocolate in party stores.
They are easy to make and look
very impressive. Even special
little fairies can help.*

❋ Melt the chocolate in double boiler over water
until of pouring consistency. Use a teaspoon to
spoon into the molds and let harden in refrigerator until set. Unmold by flexing the molds.
Although I have two antique copper molds in
the shape of lions, I find they are not as easy to
unmold as the plastic molds.

❋ Serve on an elevated cake stand surrounded
by the madeleines.

Yields: 24 chocolate animals.

Fairy Angel Food Delight

12	lemon rose geranium leaves, washed and dried
¾	cup confectioners' sugar
1	cup cake flour
12	egg whites from extra-large eggs
1½	teaspoons cream of tartar
¼	teaspoon salt
¾	cup granulated sugar
1	teaspoon vanilla extract
	Grated zest of 1 lemon
	Fresh berries and rose geranium leaves for garnish

❀ Preheat oven to 375 degrees F. Line bottom of 10-inch angel food pan with geranium leaves. Sift confectioners' sugar and cake flour together twice.

❀ In large mixer bowl combine egg whites, cream of tartar, and salt. Whisk at low speed, increasing to high until soft peaks form. Gradually add the granulated sugar and whisk until whites hold stiff peaks. Fold in the vanilla, sifted confectioners' sugar, cake flour and lemon zest. Lightly spoon into cake pan. Bake for 30 to 35 minutes or until golden and top springs back when lightly touched.

❀ Invert pan on a funnel or bottle until completely cold. Use a sharp knife around the sides of the pan and the center to release the cake. Invert on cake stand. Remove bottom of pan. Garnish with fresh geranium leaves and berries.

Yields: 12 servings.

Lemon rose geranium lends a lovely scent to this angel food cake. I used the stencil of an angel that said, "Grandma's little angel," to dust the top with confectioners' sugar.

Lime Curd Tarts

Pastry:

1⅔	cups unbleached flour
1	tablespoon granulated sugar
	Pinch of salt
	Grated zest of 1 lime
4	ounces unsalted butter, frozen
1	egg
2	tablespoons ice water

Lime Curd:

3	ounces unsalted butter
1	cup granulated sugar
3	limes, grated zest and juice
4	large eggs, beaten well
	Fresh berries and fruit for garnish

❀ Place flour, sugar and salt with zest in work bowl of food processor with steel blade. Pulse to blend. Add butter, cut into 8 equal pieces; pulse until dough is size of pebbles. Whisk egg with ice water and with food processor running, pour down spout and run just to blend. May take a bit more of ice water to bring dough together. Remove from food processor and wrap in plastic wrap. Chill for 30 minutes.

❀ Preheat oven to 375 degrees F. Roll pastry out on lightly floured marble or wooden surface to ⅛-inch thinness. Use a fluted round 1½-inch pastry cutter. Cut and place in mini-size muffin pans. Bake blind with parchment paper weighted with pie weights or dried beans. Bake 8 to 10 minutes, until golden. Remove from oven and unmold on wire rack to cool.

❀ Place butter in top of double boiler over medium high heat and when melted, whisk in sugar, zest and juice. Beat in eggs gradually and whisk over the heat until mixture thickens. Remove from heat, strain and cool.

❀ To serve, fill each pastry tart with lime curd and garnish with fresh berries or sliced fruit.

Yields: 4 dozen tarts.

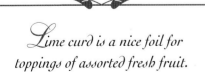

Lime curd is a nice foil for toppings of assorted fresh fruit.

Chinese Dim Sum Tea

"When I drink tea, I am conscious of peace. The cool breath of Heaven rises in my sleeves, and blows my cares away."

Lotung, Chinese poet.

I was fortunate to have a Malaysian Chinese neighbor in London who introduced me to dim sum. When she moved to Hong Kong and I was living back in Texas, she invited me to visit. My husband said it was ok on one condition, that I attend a Chinese cooking school. She found three and one had a dim sum class taught by top restaurant chefs in Chinese. I could follow their techniques but she did the translation for these wonderful tea snacks.

Dim sum are served for breakfast right until three o'clock in the afternoon in the teahouses. Many varieties are served from the dim sum carts that pass from table to table. My host told me dim sum means Yam Cha, "from the heart." I consumed thirteen varieties in one sitting before I boarded my plane to return home.

Chinese Dim Sum Tea

Hai Shao Mai

Shau Jeudz

Roast Pork Filling

Stuffed Mushrooms with Seasonal Vegetable

Cheng Du Dumplings

Fried Sesame Rice Balls

Jasmine Tea

Hai Shao Mai

½   cup ground pork

½   cup chopped crabmeat

¼   cup bamboo shoots, minced

1   green onion, minced

1   teaspoon salt

1   tablespoon cornstarch

½   teaspoon sugar

1   large egg

    Dash of white pepper

½   teaspoon sesame oil

1   dozen shrimp, peeled, cut in half lengthwise

4   water chestnuts, thinly sliced

2   dozen wonton skins

 Using a Chinese cleaver, mince pork and crabmeat; add bamboo shoots, green onion, salt, cornstarch, sugar, egg, pepper, and sesame oil, stirring to combine.

Put 1 teaspoon filling on wonton skin and pinch together in middle, leaving the top open. Decorate tops with shrimp and water chestnuts. Place on wax paper squares in bamboo steamer over water.

Steam 15 minutes in bamboo steamer set over water in a wok. Serve with soy sauce.

Yields: 24 hai shao mai.

Upon my return to the States, my luggage was thoroughly searched and when the custom agents found my cleavers and steamers, they took me into a private room to continue their interrogation. I finally convinced them I had gone there to take Chinese cooking classes. This recipe was worth the effort.

Shau Jeudz

Basic Yeast Dough:

1	**tablespoon yeast**
2	**cups water, divided**
3	**tablespoons granulated sugar, divided**
6	**cups all-purpose flour**
2	**teaspoons baking powder**
2	**tablespoons lard**

> *Making the basic yeast dough takes a bit of time but the result is light and delicious. When I was host to a master chef from Taiwan, he made these using biscuit dough out of a can.*

Shau Jeudz Filling:

4	**tablespoons vegetable cooking oil**
1	**tablespoon chopped garlic**
10	**ounces lean pork, chopped fine**
1	**pound Chinese cabbage, cooked and chopped**
1	**tablespoon light soy sauce**
	Pinch granulated sugar
1	**tablespoon chopped green onion**
¼	**teaspoon ground white pepper**

❀ Proof yeast in ¼ cup lukewarm water with 1 teaspoon sugar. Sift flour into mixing bowl with sugar and baking powder; rub in lard and add rest of water and yeast, mixing well. Knead dough until smooth and elastic. Let rise 10 minutes.

❀ Form into a long sausage roll and cut into 20 equal pieces. On a floured surface, flatten with palm of hand and roll into 4-inch pieces.

❀ Place filling in the middle, pleat edges of circle and gather up to form a round bun. Place on squares of white parchment paper in bamboo rack of steamer and let rise 10 minutes. Place over boiling water and steam for 10 to 15 minutes, depending on type of filling inside which can be shau jeudz, BBQ pork or lotus paste.

❀ Heat wok, add oil, heat to smoke; add garlic, pork and cabbage with soy sauce, sugar, green onion and seasonings. Stir-fry to mix and place in strainer to cool. Divide into 20 portions and fill buns.

Yields: 20 buns.

Roast Pork Filling

12	ounces Chinese barbecued pork
1	tablespoon vegetable cooking oil
2	green onions, minced
1	tablespoon minced gingerroot
¼	cup water
1½	tablespoons oyster sauce
1	teaspoon sesame oil
2	tablespoons cornstarch, dissolved in 2 tablespoons water

❀ Dice pork. Heat 1 tablespoon oil in wok and stir-fry onions and ginger. Add water and seasonings; bring to boil. Stir in cornstarch mixture and cook until thickened. Cool. Now add the pork and mix well.

❀ Divide into 20 portions and fill yeast buns.

Yields: 20 buns.

You can purchase the roast pork in a Chinese market.

Stuffed Mushrooms with Seasonal Filling

16	large dried Chinese mushrooms
¼	teaspoon white pepper
1	teaspoon salt
1	teaspoon egg white
½	teaspoon sesame oil
8	ounces shelled raw, deveined shrimp
8	ounces ground pork
4	water chestnuts, finely chopped
6	cups water
2	tablespoons cooking oil
1	teaspoon baking soda
1	pound bok choy or Chinese greens

Sauce:

3	tablespoons Chinese fermented black beans
2	tablespoons granulated sugar
4	tablespoons cooking oil, divided
1	teaspoon red chili pepper
1	teaspoon chopped garlic
2	tablespoons minced green onions
1	teaspoon minced gingerroot
1	cup water or chicken stock
½	teaspoon sesame oil
½	teaspoon dark soy sauce or oyster sauce
1	tablespoon cornstarch, dissolved in 1 tablespoon water

❀ Pour 1 cup boiling water over mushrooms in bowl and let reconstitute for 30 minutes. Remove any stems of mushrooms.

❀ Combine white pepper, salt, egg white and oil in a bowl and marinate mushrooms for 10 minutes. Marinate shrimp in seasoning for 15 minutes; remove and chop finely. Place in bowl and add the pork plus the finely chopped water chestnuts.

❀ Stuff mushrooms with mixture and steam in bamboo steamer for 10 minutes.

❀ Bring 6 cups water to a boil, add the oil, baking soda, salt and bok choy. Cook for 3 minutes. Drain and place on serving plate. Arrange stuffed mushrooms on top. May be served as is, or with the following sauce which gives a sheen.

❀ Steam beans with sugar and oil for 3 minutes. Heat 1 tablespoon cooking oil and stir-fry chili pepper, garlic, green onions, gingerroot and steamed black beans for 1 minute. Add remaining ingredients and bring to a boil.

Yields: 18 mushrooms.

The stuffing enhances the mushrooms and is worth the effort.

Cheng du Dumplings

8	ounces pork, 50% lean and 50% fat
2	tablespoons rice wine
1	teaspoon salt
2	tablespoons soy sauce
1	teaspoon granulated sugar
2	tablespoons cold water
1	green onion, minced

Dumpling Skins:

2	cups all-purpose flour
1	cup boiling water
1	tablespoon cold water

 Mince pork in food processor with rice wine, salt, soy sauce and sugar. Remove to a bowl and add the cold water; stir with a pair of chopsticks mixing in the minced green onion. Chill the mixture until ready to use.

 Place filling in skins and moisten edges with cold water. Bring opposite edges together, pleating the top edge. Pinch to seal. Steam 8 to 10 minutes in bamboo steamer.

 Stir boiling water into sifted flour and mix well. Use cold water to wet hands and knead dough on floured board until soft. Roll into a sausage shape; divide into 24 pieces. Roll thinly into rounds and fill. Steam on cabbage leaves.

Yields: 24 dumplings.

A trip to Mainland China in the early 1980's took me to Cheng du where I tasted these firsthand. The highlight of my Earthwatch trip was to see the Panda bears munching bamboo.

Fried Sesame Rice Balls

8	ounces glutinous rice powder
½	cup granulated sugar
1	teaspoon baking powder
½	cup lard
⅓	cup cold water
4	ounces lotus paste or red bean paste, sweet
1	egg white
1	tablespoon cold water
4	ounces sesame seed
	Vegetable oil to deep fry

❀ Mix rice flour with sugar and baking powder; cut in lard with pastry blender. Make a volcano in center and add the water. Combine to form a ball. Knead until soft. Roll into a sausage shape and cut into 24 pieces. Roll and flatten each piece.

❀ Place ½ teaspoon filling of lotus paste on flattened dough and pinch to close; rolling in wet hands to form a ball.

❀ Beat egg white and water together with chopsticks. Dip ball in egg mixture and then in sesame seeds. Roll again to be sure seeds adhere. Fry in oil heated to 375 degrees F. in wok until golden. Drain on paper towels.

Yields: 24 balls.

Save these for dessert as they are sweet. I once made these, instead of a birthday cake, for my best friend's birthday as she consumed a lot on our trip to mainland China.

Tea Punches

For entertaining with a tea based punch, think of presenting your refreshing brew in a punch bowl with an ice ring or block. Fill your mold one-third full with cold water and freeze. Arrange fresh edible flowers, such as pansies or rose petals, fresh citrus fruit slices on the ice and freeze to set the garnish in place. Carefully fill with cold water and freeze overnight. For a graduation tea, we froze several of these. I find ice blocks last a bit longer. It is easy to slip an ice ring in a punch, but an ice block should be placed in the bowl before the liquids to avoid any spillage. Ice cubes may be frozen with a strawberry in each.

Sugar Syrup

2 **cups cold water**

2 **cups granulated sugar**

❋ Combine water and sugar in a saucepan and boil until clear. This may also be accomplished in the microwave. Once the syrup has cooled, it may be stored in the refrigerator covered for ages. One of my very favorite iced tea punches uses Black Currant as the base.

An easy way to sweeten punches is to make a simple sugar syrup and keep it refrigerated.

Sparkling Black Currant Tea Punch

3	tablespoons Black Currant loose tea
6	cups boiling water
3	lemons, juiced
1	cup simple sugar syrup
¼	cup black currant liquor
1	bottle domestic champagne or carbonated water
	Chilled whole strawberries for garnish

Brew tea 5 minutes, strain and chill. Add lemon juice, simple sugar syrup and black currant liquor to tea. To serve, place an ice ring in punch bowl and pour over tea mixture. Add champagne or carbonated water. Serve in stemmed glasses with a strawberry in each glass.

Yields: 20 servings, 4 ounces each.

This is a fragrant and sweet tea before you even add the sugar syrup.

Rose Petal Champagne Punch

3	tablespoons Ceylon loose tea
6	cups boiling water
1	cup simple sugar syrup
2	oranges, juiced
¼	cup orange liqueur
1	bottle rosé wine, chilled
1	bottle pink domestic champagne, chilled

Brew tea 5 minutes, strain and chill. In punch bowl, combine brewed tea, simple sugar syrup, orange juice, orange liqueur, rosé wine and champagne.

Yields: 25 servings, 4 ounces each.

This is a lovely punch I used for a wedding reception tea. The day before, freeze a decorative ice block with edible pesticide-free pink rose petals. With scissors, snip off the base of the petals as it imparts a bitter taste.

Southwest Spiced Tea Punch

3	family size tea bags
6	cups boiling water
3	sticks cinnamon, broken in pieces
	Orange rind and lemon rind, studded with 6 cloves
2	tablespoons chopped opal basil
1	orange, juiced
1	lemon, juiced
	Sugar to taste

Brew the tea in a large non-reactive pot and infuse with the cinnamon, citrus rinds with the cloves, and the opal basil. Strain into a punch bowl with an ice ring and add the citrus juices and sugar to taste.

Yields: 15 servings, 4 ounces each.

Note: The addition of 4 ounces of tequila results in a smooth punch. However, you may wish to add 1 tablespoon per cup as each guest is served.

Opal basil is a wonderful herb used in Southwest cuisine and imparts a nice flavor.

Strawberry Tea Punch

3	tablespoons Earl Grey loose tea
6	cups boiling water
3	lemons, juiced
1	cup sugar syrup
12	mint leaves
1	liter bottled carbonated water
	Strawberries, halved

Brew tea 5 minutes, strain and chill. Pour over ice ring in punch bowl and add lemon juice, sugar syrup and bruised mint leaves. Add carbonated water last. Serve in clear cups with strawberry half in each.

Yields: 25 servings, 4 ounces each.

Strawberries and Earl Grey are a perfect match for this punch.

Cranberry Iced Tea Punch

3   ounces dried cranberries

3   tablespoons Ceylon loose tea

6   cups boiling water

⅓   cup granulated sugar

2   cups cranberry juice cocktail, chilled

1   (6-ounce) can frozen orange juice concentrate

1   (28-ounce) bottle ginger ale or cranberry flavored water

❀ Make an ice block with dried cranberries the day before. Brew the tea 5 minutes, strain and chill. In punch bowl, combine tea with sugar, cranberry juice and orange juice concentrate adding the ginger ale last. Serve in punch cups.

Yields: 25 servings, 4 ounces each.

Note: Grand Marnier may be added if alcohol is desired.

Cranberries and oranges are a classic combination for flavor.

Hot Rum Tea Punch

3	tablespoons Darjeeling tea
6	cups boiling water
2	sticks cinnamon, broken in pieces
	Rind of 1 orange and 1 lemon, studded with 6 whole cloves
	Juices of 1 orange and 1 lemon
1	cup dark rum
	Honey, to taste

Infuse the tea with the cinnamon and citrus rinds. Strain into a copper pot that may be used for serving and kept warm over a burner. Add the citrus juices, rum and sweeten with the honey. Serve warm in mugs.

Yields: 12 servings, 4 ounces each.

This is wonderful during the holiday season as it imparts a rosy glow to one's appearance.

Spiced Tea Punch

2	quarts water
½	cup Darjeeling loose tea
2	teaspoons whole cloves
2	teaspoons whole allspice
2	cinnamon sticks, broken up
	Rinds from 1 lemon and 1 orange
6	slices gingerroot
1	cup sugar syrup

❀ In non-reactive saucepan, bring water to boil. Add the tea, cloves, allspice, cinnamon sticks, citrus rinds and gingerroot. Cover and simmer 5 minutes. Strain into large punch bowl and sweeten with sugar syrup. Serve warm.

Yields: 15 servings, 4 ounces each.

Note: For an added kick, add 1 cup fruit flavored brandy. The sugar syrup may be made two weeks in advance but the punch is to made the day of the event and warmed for serving. A large copper pot makes a nice container with a ladle.

With so many holiday tea blends available, you may choose not to do this one, but it is a winner.

Brewing Tea for a Crowd

1   **cup loose tea or 12 tea bags**

1   **gallon water**

❀ Place tea in a non-reactive container. Bring 1 quart of water to a full boil at 212 degrees F. Pour over tea, cover and steep 7 minutes. Strain tea and add 3 quarts of water brought to 190 degrees F.

Yields: 25 cups.

Note: For 50 cups, use 1½ cups of loose tea and 2 gallons of water. Brew the same way as above.

You can make your own tea bag, either of coffee filters or from a cheesecloth about 20 inches square. Tie with a string allowing room for the tea to expand. You may retrieve your tea bag if you allow for a long string and attach it to the side of your brewing container.

This is the recipe from a Lipton's brochure.

Mincemeat Tarts

Pastry:

2	cups unbleached all-purpose flour
2	tablespoons ground almonds
4	tablespoons granulated sugar
	Grated rind of 1 lemon
6	ounces unsalted butter
1	large egg yolk
3	tablespoons cream

Mincemeat:

1	pound raisins
1	pound sultanas
1	pound dried currants
4	ounces mixed candied peel
1	orange, quartered and deseeded
1	lemon, quartered and deseeded
1	pound tart apples
1	cup fresh seedless red grapes
½	cup slivered almonds
1	pound dark brown sugar, divided
1	teaspoon ground cinnamon
1	teaspoon ground nutmeg
1	teaspoon ground cloves
1	teaspoon ground mace
1	cup sherry
1	cup cognac or rum

❧ Combine flour, almonds, sugar and lemon rind in food processor. Add butter and pulse to combine. Whisk egg yolk with cream and add to mixture. Turn out on plastic wrap and refrigerate for 30 minutes.

> *A British Cordon Bleu trained cook invited us for an English New Year's Eve party and she had these spilling down the shelves of one wall. I persuaded her to share her recipe for the pastry. The mincemeat is my own.*

❧ In food processor, chop all fruit and almonds 2 cups at a time with ½ cup of the brown sugar. Mix spices with sherry and add to the mixture along with the cognac. Place in gallon jar and age at least a month in cool place or refrigerator.

Yields: 2 quarts mincemeat.

❧ Preheat oven to 375 degrees F. Roll pastry out on floured surface. Cut 2½-inch pastry circles and put in tart pans. Fill with 1 tablespoon of mincemeat. Dampen edges of pastry with cold water and place pastry circle on top of mincemeat. Pierce center with sharp knife. Sprinkle top of tart with granulated sugar. Bake for 15 minutes or until golden. Remove from oven to cooling rack.

Yields: 18 tarts.

Dresdner Stollen

8	ounces raisins, golden and dark mixed
8	ounces candied orange peel
8	ounces mixed candied fruit
¼	cup rum

* Marinate fruit in rum overnight in a mixing bowl.

3	packages active dry yeast
1	teaspoon granulated sugar
1	pound unbleached flour
1	cup lukewarm water

* In mixing bowl, place yeast, sugar, flour and water; mix with paddle. Set aside to rise until double.

10	ounces unsalted butter, softened
3	ounces brown sugar
2	ounces almond paste
1	large egg

* In mixing bowl, combine butter, brown sugar, almond paste and egg; mix with paddle and set aside.

1	pound, 6 ounces unbleached flour
1	teaspoon salt
½	teaspoon ground cardamom
½	teaspoon ground nutmeg
½	teaspoon ground cinnamon
½	teaspoon ground cloves

* Sift flour, salt and spices together. In mixing bowl, place first yeast mixture and add half of the flour, salt and spices, mixing well. Add the butter, almond paste, egg and sugar mixture. Add rest of flour and spice mixture. Knead the fruit mixture into dough. Cover and let rise 1 hour in warm place. Dough will be firm.

| 4 | ounces unsalted butter, melted. |
| ½ | cup vanilla flavored granulated sugar |

🌼 Work dough into 1-pound balls until dough does not tear. Roll out and using rolling pen, press a bend down just to the front of the stollen to make a crease in dough. Bring ends of stollen together to form a quarter moon.

🌼 Let rise until not quite double. Bake in preheated 350 degree F oven for 25 to 30 minutes. Remove from oven and using a clean tea towel to hold the stollen, douse in melted butter twice and sprinkle with vanilla sugar.

Yields: 5 stollen.

Note: To make vanilla sugar, bury a vanilla bean in 2 cups of granulated sugar for a week.

I was fortunate to have Bruno Leutsinger teach some pastry and bread classes for me when he moved here from San Francisco, where he taught classes for James Beard at The Stanford Court. He was a marvelous teacher. I make this stollen every Christmas for gifts.

Buche de Noel

9	**large eggs**
1	**cup plus 2 tablespoons granulated sugar**
1	**cup all-purpose flour**
1	**tablespoon unsalted butter, melted**

✿ Preheat oven to 400 degrees F. Place parchment paper on 11 x 16-inch jelly-roll pan allowing for a 2-inch box of parchment at each end of pan. Butter and flour pan, shaking out excess flour.

✿ Whisk the eggs in mixing bowl and add the sugar, whipping to a ribbon stage or lay your finger down on top of batter. If crease does not run together, batter is ready for rest of ingredients. Fold in the flour lightly and melted butter last. Spread evenly on parchment paper and bake for 8 to 10 minutes; do not over bake or cake will crack.

✿ Remove from oven to cooling rack. Sprinkle sugar on top of cake and place parchment over the cake. Place a baking sheet over the cake and turn out. Very carefully, peel off the parchment paper and use a serrated knife to slice off any dry part along the sides. Roll cake up in parchment paper. You may freeze the cake now, tightly wrapped, or place in your refrigerator for 3 days.

✿ Make meringue mushrooms for decoration and fill roulade with butter cream.

Note: For chocolate roulade, substitute 1 ounce of cocoa powder for 1 ounce of the flour.

Meringue Mushrooms:

1	**large egg white**
¼	**cup granulated sugar**

✿ Preheat oven to 200 degrees F. Line baking sheet with parchment paper.

✿ In mixing bowl, whisk egg white until stiff. Add 1 teaspoon sugar, beat, and fold in rest of sugar. Fit pastry bag with ¼-inch plain tube; fill with meringue. Pipe mushrooms and stems onto parchment lined pan. Dry in oven 50 to 60 minutes. Remove from oven and cool.

Butter Cream Frosting:

½	cup granulated sugar
2	tablespoons water
2	large egg yolks
6	ounces unsalted butter, softened

Assembly:

½	cup red currant jelly
	Green food coloring
1	tablespoon powdered instant coffee
12	ounces semi-sweet and extra bittersweet chocolate

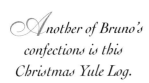

Another of Bruno's confections is this Christmas Yule Log.

✤ In pan, bring sugar and water to boil; boil until clear, about 3 minutes. Place egg yolks in mixing bowl with whisk. Slowly add syrup, beating. Beat 5 minutes to cool syrup.

✤ Add butter, 1 tablespoon at a time beating well. Cover and refrigerate.

✤ Unwrap cake and spread with red currant jelly; may need to warm in microwave. Roll cake up again.

✤ To 2 tablespoons of the butter cream, add few drops of green food coloring to make leaves.

✤ Dissolve instant coffee in ½ teaspoon warm water and stir into ⅓ third cup of the butter cream.

✤ Melt chocolate over hot water and stir into remaining butter cream.

✤ Slice ends off cake at a diagonal. Use spatula to spread chocolate cream over top and sides of roulade but not the ends. Use tines of a fork to simulate bark by pulling down the length of the roulade.

✤ Pipe circles on ends of cake with the dark chocolate cream and place on top of cake like knobs of wood. Use pastry bag with leaf tip to pipe ivy over the log with the green cream.

✤ Use the chocolate cream to glue the stem of the mushroom to the cap. Garnish with meringue mushrooms that are dusted with cocoa.

✤ You may color coconut green for grass or dust log with powdered sugar for snowy look.

Yields: 10 servings.

Rum Plum Cake

½	**cup prunes, roughly chopped**
¼	**cup rum**
½	**cup sultanas**
¼	**cup candied fruit mix**
¼	**cup glacéed cherries, halved**
2½	**cups all-purpose flour, divided**
8	**ounces unsalted butter, softened**
1	**cup dark brown sugar**
4	**large eggs**
¼	**cup black molasses**
1	**lemon, zest and juice**
1	**teaspoon baking soda**
¼	**teaspoon salt**
1	**teaspoon mixed spices, cinnamon, cloves, nutmeg**

❁ Soak prunes with rum overnight. In large bowl, mix together the dried fruits and half the flour to coat the fruits with the flour.

❁ Preheat oven to 325 degrees F. Butter and line the bottom of a 10-inch round deep baking pan.

❁ In mixing bowl, cream the butter and slowly add the sugar beating until light in color. Beat in the eggs, one at a time; then the molasses and the lemon juice with the zest. Add the rest of the flour that has been sifted with the soda and spices. Combine with the fruit mixture. Turn out into the baking tin and bake for 1 hour. Turn oven down to 275 degrees F. and bake 30 to 45 minutes more. Remove from oven and cool in pan on a wire rack.

❁ May store cake in a tin for 1 month or may freeze it.

Yields: 20 servings.

The English excel at sticky, fruity cakes and this recipe came from my PHD neighbor, Marvelous, as my husband called her as he could never pronounce her Welsh name, Morphyd.

The Tea Tasting Alphabet

If one wishes to talk about tea, one needs to learn the language of tea. Some of the following terms describe the dry leaf while others describe the infused leaf and the brewed liquor.

Agony of the leaves: This takes place when boiling water is poured over the leaves.

Aroma: Refers to the smell of tea, be it pleasant or fragrant, like a flower.

Astringency: The tea's liquor may be piquant when tasted.

Body: Refers to whether a tea feels full, thick or thin in the mouth.

Bright: A sparkling characteristic of all fine teas' liquors.

Character: A desired quality of well-harvested leaves, grown at high altitudes of 4-7,000 feet.

Dull: Describes a leaf with no sheen or gloss.

Earthy: Describes a flavor that is the result of the soil in which the plant is grown.

Flat: Refers to a tea lacking in briskness and bite, usually due to its age.

Fruity: A characteristic of oolongs.

Hard: Refers to a very pungent brew.

Harsh: A very rough taste due to underwithered leaves.

Lacking: Describes a liquor that has no body.

Light: Refers to a brew that lacks color and strength.

Malty: A desirable characteristic that is subtle. Found in Assam teas.

Mature: Tea that is not flat or bitter in taste.

Metallic: A taste that is coppery.

Muscatel: A desirable flavor found in Darjeelings. Like a muscatel grape.

Muddy: A dull tea in appearance.

Nose: The smell of the dry leaf just as wine has a nose.

Powdery: A fine light tea dust that is unpleasant.

Pungent: Strength, briskness and brightness which are highly desirable.

Quality: Refers to how the cup tastes.

Rasping: A very harsh, coarse liquor.

Smoky: A desirable flavor of some Chinese teas, such as Lapsang Souchong which is smoked over pine.

Soft: Poor firing during fermentation results in any taste of briskness.

Stale: Old tea whose flavor and aroma has faded due to age or improper storage.

Stewy: Bitter tasting tea that has been steeped too long or the leaves have been improperly fired.

Tannin: Astringent chemical constituent of tea.

Tippy: Teas with a generous amount of budding leaf, white or golden tips.

Toasty: Highly fired teas have this, particularly Keemun.

Weedy: A grassy taste due to underwithering.

Winey: Some teas have this desirable quality. Darjeeling is the red wine of teas.

Mail-Order Sources

American Classic Tea
6617 Maybank Hwy.
PO Box 12810
Wadmalaw Island, SC 29487
(800) 443-5987

Angelina
226 Rue de Rivoli
75001 Paris, France
R.C. Bigelow, Inc.
201 Black Rock Turnpike
Fairfield, Ct. 06432-55512
(800) 841-8158

Bramah Tea & Coffee Museum
The Clove Building
Maguire Street
London SE1 2NQ, Great Britain
(44) 0171 378 0222

Celestial Seasonings
4600 Sleepytime Dr.
Boulder, Co. 80301-3292
(303) 530-5300

Corti Brothers
5810 Folsom Blvd.
PO Box 191358
Sacramento, Ca. 95819
(916) 736-3800

The Cultured Cup
5346 Beltline Road
Dallas, Tx. 75254
(972) 960 1521
(888) 847 8327

Dean & Deluca
560 Broadway
New York, NY 10012
(212) 431-1691

Eastern Shore Company
PO Box 84
Church Hill, MD 21623
(800) 542-6064

Fauchon
422 Park Avenue
New York, NY 10022
(212) 308-5919

Fauchon
1000 Madison Avenue
New York, NY 10022
(212)570-2271

Fauchon
28 Place de La Madeleine
75008 Paris, France
7.42 .60.11

Fortnum & Mason Ltd.
181 Piccadilly
London, W1A 1ER
UK

Grace Rare Teas
Grace Tea Company, Ltd.
50 West 17th St.
New York, NY 10011
(212) 255-2935

Harney & Sons
Village Green
PO. Box 638
Salisbury, CT. 06068
(800) 832-8463

Imperial Tea Court
1411 Powell Street
San Francisco, Ca. 94133
(415) 788-6080

Itoen
822 Madison Avenue
New York, NY 10021
(212) 988-7111

Mariage Frères
30-32 Rue du Bourg-Tiborg
75004 Paris, France
42.72.28.11

Mariage Frères
13 Rue des Grands Augustins
75006 Paris, France
40.51.82.50

Murchie's
5580 Parkwood Way
Richmond, B.C.
Canada V6V2M4
(604) 231-7422

Simpson & Vail
53 Park Place
New York, NY 10007
(800) 282-8327

The Sir Thomas Lipton Collection
115 Brand Road
Salem, Va. 24156
(703) 389-8336

Twinings
216 The Strand
London, WC2
UK

Upton Tea Imports
PO Box 159
Upton, Ma. 01568
(800) 234-832

Verlet
256 Rue Saint-Honoré
75001 Paris, France
42.60.67.39

Mark T. Wendell
PO Box 1312
West Concord, Ma. 01742
(508) 369-3709

Metric Conversions

Weight Equivalents *(approximate)*

¼ ounce .... 7 grams

½ ounce .... 15 grams

1 ounce .... 30 grams

2 ounces .... 60 grams

3 ounces .... 90 grams

4 ounces .... 115 grams

5 ounces .... 150 grams

6 ounces .... 175 grams

7 ounces .... 200 grams

8 ounces (½ pound) .... 225 grams

9 ounces .... 250 grams

10 ounces .... 300 grams

11 ounces .... 325 grams

12 ounces .... 350 grams

13 ounces .... 375 grams

14 ounces .... 400 grams

15 ounces .... 425 grams

1 pound .... 450 grams

1 pound, 2 ounces .... 500 grams

1½ pounds .... 750 grams

2 pounds .... 900 grams

2¼ pounds .... 1 kilogram

3 pounds .... 1.4 kilograms

4 pounds .... 1.8 kilograms

4½ pounds .... 2 kilograms

Volume equivalents *(approximate)*

¼ teaspoon .... 1.25 milliliters

½ teaspoon .... 2.5 milliliters

1 teaspoon .... 5 milliliters

½ tablespoon .... 7.5 milliliters

1 tablespoon .... 15 milliliters

¼ cup .... 60 milliliters

⅓ cup .... 75 milliliters

½ cup .... 125 milliliters

⅔ cup .... 150 milliliters

¾ cup .... 175 milliliters

1 cup .... 250 milliliters

1½ cup. .... 300 milliliters

1 pint .... 500 milliliters

2½ cups...................... 625 milliliters

1 quart........................ 1 liter

Oven Temperature Equivalents

Fahrenheit	Celsius
250-275	130-140
300.............................	150
325.............................	170
350.............................	180
375.............................	190
400.............................	200
425.............................	220
450.............................	230
475.............................	250

Acknowledgements

I wish to thank .....

The first person who suggested I teach a class on A Proper English Tea is my daughter, Emily Snyder, and I shall be forever grateful to her.

Rodney Tyler, the British journalist, who insisted I write a book on tea and etiquette at our very first meeting back in 1990. Rod wrote the foreword for this book only five days before he had a fatal heart attack.

Karen Davis, wife of Gerald Davis, who generously gave her permission for the use of Gerry's wonderful photo of a tea in my back garden.

Angela Galloway-Marshall, my British friend, who allowed me to hold my very first tea class in her home. Over a brewed pot of Fortnum & Mason tea, this talented artist and I finalized the book's cover. Angela also lent several of her tea antiques for the photos and designed the Fairy Tea Invitation.

Gail Greene, an outstanding food stylist, lent her expertise to the fabulous shots of the tea fare making it eye-appealing—even those gray sardine sandwiches.

Linda Attaway, my assistant for many years, cheefully came to make sandwiches as well as clear up.

Shari Carlson of Dessert Dreams created the purple butterflies for the Fairy Tea.

John Parrish, the photographer, who brought my tea fare to life in his extraordinary photos.

Martha Aufricht, who lent her brass samovar for the tea equipage layout.

Gladys Howard, my college roommate, allowed me to use her tea urn and accessories for the Queen's Tea.

Flo Braker, whom I met through IACP and who mentored me through the years prior to publication.

Lisa Ekus, who suggested a change in the title to **Tea Time Entertaining**.

Rich Snyder, my son, for helping me setup more than once for tea demonstrations.

Janiece Snyder, my daughter-in-law, for sharing her love of gardens, flowers and photography.

Mom and Dad, who taught me the joys of the table.

Richard Snyder, my tea partner for life, who took me to the land of tea drinkers never suspecting where it would lead. He has been a terrific support and my computer guru throughout the writing of this book.

To all the thousands of students who kept asking for more tea themes and recipes which resulted in a plethora of ideas for the manuscript.

Bibliography

Blofield, John. *The Chinese Art of Tea*. Boston; Shambhala Publications, Inc., 1985.

Bramah, Edward. *Novelty Teapots*. London; Quiller Press, 1992.

Burgess, Anthony; Stella, Alan; Beautheac, Nadine; Brochard, Giles; Donzel, Catherine. *The Book of Tea*. Paris; Flammarion.

Chow, Kit and Kramer, Ione. *All the Tea in China*. San Francisco; China Books & Periodicals, 1990.

Foley, Tricia. *Having Tea*. New York; Clarkson N. Potter, Inc., 1987.

Huxley, Gervas. *Talking of Tea*. Ivyland, Pa.; John Wagner & Sons Inc, 1956.

Johnson, Dorothea. *Tea & Etiquette*. Washington; Capital Books, 1998.

Mitscher, Lester A. and Dolby, Victoria. *The Green Tea Book*. Garden City Park, New York; Avery Publishing Group, 1998.

Pettigrew, Jane. *A Social History of Tea*. Great Britain; The National Trust, 2001.

Pettigrew, Jane. *The Tea Companion*. London; Apple Press, 1997.

Pratt, James Norwood and Rosen, Diana. *The Tea Lover's Companion*. New York; Carol Publishing Group, 1995.

Pratt, James Norwood. *New Tea Lover's Treasury*. San Francisco; Publishing Technology Associates, 1999.

Pratt, James Norwood. *The Tea Lover's Treasury*. San Francisco; 101 Productions, 1982.

Pruess, Joanna with Harney, John. *Eat Tea*. Guilford, Connecticut; The Lyons Press, 2001.

Repplier, Agnes. *To Think of Tea*. Boston and New York; Houghton Mifflin Company, 1932

Shalleck, Jamie. *Tea*. New York; The Viking Press, 1972.

Smith, Michael. *The Afternoon Tea Book*. New York; Atheneum, 1986.

Tanaka, Sen'o. *The Tea Ceremony*. Tokyo, New York and London; Kodansha International, 1973.

Ukers, William H. *The Romance of Tea*. New York and London; A. Knopf, 1936.

Wedgwood, Barbara. *Three Centuries of Wedgwood*. Dallas, Texas; The Jarvis Press, 1993.

Index

Tea Time Thoughts

Tea Time Thoughts

Tea Time Thoughts

Tea Time Thoughts

_____

_____

_____

_____

_____

_____

_____

_____

_____

_____

_____

_____

_____

_____

_____

_____

Tea Time Thoughts